DA VINCI CODE DECODED

Martin Lunn

disinformation

Published by:
The Disinformation Company Ltd.
163 Third Avenue, Suite 108
New York, NY 10003
Tel.: +1.212.691.1605
Fax: +1.212.473.8096
www.disinfo.com

Design & Layout:Browns/New York
www.brownsdesign.com
Library of Congress Control Number: 2004100535
ISBN: 0-9729529-7-7
Printed in USA

Distributed in USA and Canada by:
Consortium Book Sales and Distribution
1045 Westgate Drive, Suite 90
St. Paul, MN 55114
Toll Free: +1.800.283.3572
Local: +1.651.221.9035
Fax: +1.651.221.0124
www.cbsd.com

Distributed in the United Kingdom and Eire by:
Turnaround Publisher Services Ltd.
Unit 3, Olympia Trading Estate
Coburg Road
London, N22 6TZ
Tel.: +44.(0)20.8829.3000
Fax: +44.(0)20.8881.5088
www.turnaround-uk.com

Acknowledgements

Thanks to Tracy Twyman and Brian Albert of *Dagobert's Revenge* magazine for their invaluable advice and support in researching this book, and also for introducing me to The Disinformation Company's Gary Baddeley and Richard Metzger. Gary and Richard also put in long hours helping to polish the book you now hold. I should also acknowledge the forbearance of Julio and Steve while living amongst the swirling sea of research materials that engulfed us for the months spent researching this book.

Contents

Chapter Three
The Davidic and Merovingian Bloodlines   49

Chapter Four
The Real Saunière and Rennes-le-Château   67

Chapter Five
Constantine the Great

Chapter Six
The Holy Grail in Europe

Chapter Seven
Jesus Christ – the facts and fiction

Chapter Eleven
Significant Parisian Locations Visited in *The Da Vinci Code*   137

Chapter Twelve
Rosslyn Chapel   141

Chapter Thirteen
London   151

Glossary   159

Bibliography/References   169

Index   175

Da Vinci Code Decoded

List of Photographs and illustrations

Introduction

THE QUESTION THAT HAS BEEN ON EVERYONE'S LIPS SINCE THE PUBLICATION OF *THE DA VINCI CODE* IN APRIL, 2003 IS "HOW MUCH OF WHAT HE SAYS IS TRUE?" GRANTED, AUTHOR DAN BROWN SAYS AT THE BEGINNING OF HIS NOVEL THAT "ALL DESCRIPTIONS OF ARTWORK, ARCHITECTURE, DOCUMENTS AND SECRET RITUALS IN THIS NOVEL ARE ACCURATE" BUT IT IS FICTION, AFTER ALL, AND SURELY HE'S ALLOWED JUST A LITTLE POETIC LICENSE?

The purpose of this book is to try to separate fact from fiction. It's not easy! Sometimes the subject matter that Brown uses looks a certain way from one perspective and completely different from another.

The Christian church certainly feels it is under the spotlight because of *The Da Vinci Code* – and it is not fond of being observed with a critical eye. The Church has depended upon the faith of its followers for 2000 years and conveniently for them faith is belief without evidence. Christianity has been unable to provide any convincing proof of much that it wants its followers to believe and for more than the last century has had to defend itself in the face of a variety of scientific discoveries that it wishes would just go away.

Now the Church once again finds itself facing difficult questions, this time all because of a best-selling novel called *The Da Vinci Code*.

The Da Vinci Code has been such a resounding success, not because of the admittedly engaging, but rather run-of-the-mill adventure/murder plot, but because Dan Brown has stimulated his readers to see previously accepted familiar "truths" in a totally unfamiliar light.

In so doing, he has whetted the appetites of many, yet leaves them curiously unsatisfied at the end of the novel. Brown provokes his readers into asking themselves difficult questions and I hope that this book will go at least some way towards satisfying people's developing appetite for this type of material.

Some of us think that there has been a "softening up" process over the last couple of decades to lead mankind towards some kind of spiritual revelation. This has been done through science fiction films like *The Matrix* trilogy and popular interest in and debate on esoteric phenomena as diverse as UFOs and crop circles. This revelation could even take the form of excavations at Rennes-le-Château, resulting in recognition of the Grail families.

Dan Brown's subversive novel *The Da Vinci Code* has contributed much to the change the world is going through. Are you part of this change and do you want to know more?

– Martin Lunn, Barcelona, Spain

Chapter One
Leonardo da Vinci – his life and art

DAN BROWN'S CHOICE OF LEONARDO DA VINCI AS THE ARTIST CENTRAL TO HIS BOOK AND ITS TITLE CHARACTER IS BOTH INTERESTING AND SENSIBLE. KNOWLEDGE OF LEONARDO HAS COME DOWN THROUGH THE CENTURIES TO PRACTICALLY EVERYONE IN THE WESTERN WORLD. HE IS PROBABLY THE GREATEST EXAMPLE OF UNIVERSALITY THAT THE WORLD HAS EVER KNOWN. LIKE ALBERT EINSTEIN, LEONARDO DA VINCI IS A HUMAN TRADEMARK INDICATING "GENIUS."

In his day it was by no means rare for people to dabble in more than one area of knowledge or expertise, but despite this there was not, even at that time, anyone who could match him as painter, sculptor, architect and engineer. Not only that, he explored nature so that he could gain an understanding not just of how things worked, but why. Dan Brown is right to say, therefore, that Leonardo was a "worshipper of Nature's divine order." While his contemporaries were painting plants from pictures in books, he was copying directly from nature. His choice of plants in his paintings was symbolic. As Dan Brown tells us in shocked tones, he did indeed dissect corpses: about 30 in total, averaging roughly two per year while he was studying. It was illegal, but whether he actually exhumed the bodies himself is a different matter. The Church believed that the human body had to be buried intact so that it could be resurrected in the Last Day of Judgment. Nonetheless, Leonardo appears to have had the sanction of the Church in this practice; no doubt many influential people were impressed by the skill shown in his drawings presenting the human body in various layered forms. In other words, it was forbidden to dissect corpses, but nobody could be bothered to take action

5

over Leonardo's doing so. (This apparent disregard for the law in some cases may ring bells with anyone familiar with the legal system in Italy today.) Leonardo's detailed drawings contributed greatly to the body of medicine from which we benefit today.

His inventions showed considerable vision. He drew designs for tanks, the parachute, the car and the helicopter which would not be realized for centuries. He even designed a telescope 100 years before Galileo. To Leonardo, man's highest sense organ was sight because of its ability to relay with accuracy. His philosophy was thus *saper vedere* – knowing how to see. For Dan Brown to say that Leonardo painted Christian themes as a means of commercial enterprise to fund his lavish lifestyle is, perhaps, unfair on the man. He executed everything that he did with unparalleled skill and came from an affluent background. What is true is that he never painted an interpretation of the Crucifixion. He could also hardly be described as having created an "enormous output" of Christian art; of the mere seventeen surviving paintings that can definitely be attributed to him, several are unfinished.

He is referred to by art historians simply as "Leonardo." The name "da Vinci" is not a surname; it only describes where he was from. It is similar to referring to Alexander the Great just as "the Great." However "da Vinci" is in such common use that there is no ambiguity.

Leonardo was born in 1452, the illegitimate son of Ser Piero, a successful lawyer and landlord in Florence in Italy. His mother was a Florentine peasant who later married a local workman. Leonardo was brought up on his father's estate in Vinci, near Empoli, where he was treated as a legitimate son, and it was there that he was educated in reading, writing and arithmetic. He studied Latin, higher mathematics and geometry later on.

When Leonardo was about fifteen years old, his father apprenticed him to Andrea del Verrocchio, from whom he learned painting, sculpture and technical-mechanical arts. It was at this time that he would have met another Priory of Sion Grand Master, Botticelli, who was also apprenticed to Verrocchio then. It is probable that he started his studies of anatomy at the neighboring studio during this period. He worked independently in Florence until 1481. Many of his works date from this time, including the largely unfinished *Adoration of the Magi*.

In 1482, he entered the service of Ludovico Sforza, a.k.a. Ludovico il Moro (The Moor), the Duke of Milan, where he was listed in the register of the royal household as *pictor et inegarius ducalis* ("painter and engineer of the Duke"). Sforza was a close friend of René d'Anjou, yet another Grand Master of the Priory of Sion. Leonardo spent the next seventeen years there until Ludovico fell from power. In addition to painting, sculpture and designing court festivals, he was a technical adviser in architecture, fortifications and military matters, even serving as a hydraulic and mechanical engineer. It was at this time that he developed his universal genius most fully.

During this period he completed only seven paintings, including the first version of *The Madonna of the Rocks* mentioned by Dan Brown. This was an altarpiece which would be displayed at the church of San Francesco Grande in Milan. The magnificent *The Last Supper*, which is painted on the wall of Santa Maria delle Grazie in Milan, was also painted at this time.

Leonardo then started to develop his idea of a "science of painting." He concluded that painters, using their superior ability of sight, were the perfect mediums to transfer knowledge pictorially and he therefore used his art to teach. This is particularly important to an understanding of Leonardo da Vinci's role in *The Da Vinci Code*. Leonardo did not just paint a pretty picture of The Last Supper. It was his way of telling us something of immense importance in a way that has come down the centuries to us and can be understood by anyone who has access to his code. When presenting text and illustrations together, he gave priority to the illustration. The illustration does not express the text; the text serves only to explain the picture.

Between 1490 and 1495, he wrote treatises on painting and architecture and books on the elements of mechanics and human anatomy. He also continued studying in various scientific fields. He wrote and sketched detailed accounts of everything he did, which amounts to a total of thousands of pages, many of which survive to this day.

As Leonardo was left-handed, mirror-writing was not too difficult for him. It was not an easy style to read and his spelling mistakes and abbreviations compounded the difficulty. Nor were his notes always written in a logical order. He used mirror writing throughout his work, but his correspondence to others indicates that he was also at ease with conventional handwriting. Leonardo's main biographer, Serge Bramley, has examined all of Leonardo's surviving manuscripts and concluded that he wrote with both hands in both directions.

One of the consequences, if not the reason for his use of mirror writing, was that the ink did not smudge when he wrote with his left hand. He could also, of course, have had the intention of writing secretly as he did not want others to steal his ideas. An additional reason for security could have arisen from his unconventional ideas on Christianity. As Dan Brown points out, during Leonardo's time left-handedness was associated with the "left-hand path" and satanic forces. Therefore left-handed people were regarded with suspicion; it was unusual back then to find someone who was as open about it as Leonardo. He wrote with the intention of publication and in the margins of one of his anatomy sketches he asks his followers to ensure that his works are printed.

By the beginning of 1500 Leonardo had left Milan and returned to Florence via Venice, where the governing council asked his advice on the impending Turkish invasion in Friuli. Leonardo recommended flooding the area. When back in Florence, Leonardo started a cartoon for the painting *Virgin and Child with St.Anne,* and *Madonna with the Yarn-Winder.*[1] In 1503 Leonardo left Florence and entered the service of Cesare Borgia, the Duke of Valentinois, who was the natural son of Pope Alexander VI and the most feared person of his time. He was suspected of having murdered his brother, but the crime of which he was undoubtedly guilty was the murder in August 1500 of his brother-in-law Alfonso, Duke of Bisceglie, the second husband of his infamous sister, Lucrezia. Leonardo was fascinated by Borgia, who at 27 years old was only half Leonardo's age.

At this time, Leonardo engaged himself in making city plans and topographical maps. His work formed the foundation of modern cartography. In 1503, he returned to Florence and planned a canal that would run from the city to the sea. This was never actually carried out, but there is now an expressway connecting Florence to the sea and it runs on exactly the same route as that which Leonardo proposed.

Leonardo painted the *Mona Lisa* while he was working on a mural for the Hall of the Five Hundred in Florence between the years 1503 and 1506. He left this painting unfinished when he then returned to Milan at the request of Charles d'Amboise, the Governor of the King of France in Milan. He spent the next six years in Milan, concentrating on architecture and was paid the princely sum of 400 ducats a year. He painted the second version of *The Madonna of the Rocks* at this time.

When the French were expelled from Milan in 1513, Leonardo moved to Rome. Giuliano de Medici, the brother of Pope Leo X, gave him a suite of rooms in his residence, the Belvedere, which formed part of the Vatican. He was paid, but while others such as Michelangelo were working on various architectural and artistic projects, Leonardo was left with not much to do.

[1] This painting was stolen from Drumlaring Castle in the South of Scotland in August 2003.

Leonardo was attached to the army of Charles de Montpensier et de Bourbon, the Constable of France, and the Viceroy of Languedoc and Milan, reputed to be the most powerful Lord in France in the early sixteenth century. He took over as Grand Master of the Priory of Sion after Leonardo da Vinci in 1519.

At the age of 65, Leonardo took up the offer of the young King of France, Francis I, to enter his service. He spent the last three years of his life living in a small residence at Cloux (later to be called Clos-Lucé) near the King's summer palace on the Loire River. His title was "premier peintre, architecte et méchanicien du Roi" (first painter, architect, and mechanic of the King). To a great extent he was treated as an honored guest at this time. The only painting that he managed to complete was *St. John the Baptist*, and much of the only other work that he did consisted of sketches of court festivals. He drew up a design for the palace of gardens for the King's mother, but these plans had to be abandoned because of a threat of malaria.

Leonardo da Vinci died on May 2, 1519 at Cloux and was buried at the palace church of Saint-Florentin. However, the church was badly damaged during the French Revolution and was eventually pulled down in the nineteenth century. His grave can no longer be found. His most devoted pupil, Francesco Melzi, inherited his estate.

Leonardo has been described as one of the first Rosicrucians and one biographer, Vasali, has described him as being of an "heretical state of mind." This heresy is thought to include his belief that Jesus Christ had a twin brother, Thomas. In his painting *The Last Supper*, there are what appear to be two almost identical Christ figures. The second figure from the left shows a distinct resemblance to Christ, shown seated in the center and it is suspected that this figure may represent Thomas.

Several of Leonardo's works are discussed by Robert Langdon, Sophie Neveu, Leigh Teabing and other characters in *The Da Vinci Code*. The more important ones are:

The Vitruvian Man

One of the latest appearances of da Vinci's drawing *The Vitruvian Man* (and no doubt the most widespread) is on the Italian one euro coin, indicating that the popularity of this symbol is not diminishing. It is also featured on the cover of this book. Leonardo wrote of this drawing himself that:

> Vitruvius, the architect, says in his work on architecture that the measurements of the human body are as follows: that is that 4 fingers make 1 palm, and 4 palms make 1 foot, 6 palms make 1 cubit; 4 cubits make a man's height. And 4 cubits make one pace, and 24 palms make a man. The length of a man's outspread arms is equal to his height. From the roots of his hair to the bottom of his chin is the tenth of a man's height; from the bottom of the chin to the top of the head is one eighth of his height; from the top of the breast to the roots of the hair will be the seventh part of the whole man. From the nipples to the top of the head will be the fourth part of man. The greatest width of the shoulders contains in itself the fourth part of man. From the elbow to the tip of the hand will be the fifth part of a man; and from the elbow to the angle of the armpit will be the eighth part of man. The whole hand will be the tenth part of the man. The distance from the bottom of the chin to the nose and from the roots of the hair to the eyebrows is, in each case the same, and like the ear, a third of the face.

The Notebooks of Leonardo da Vinci, Vol. 1 (of a 2 vol. set in paperback) pp. 182-3, Dover, ISBN 0-486-22572-0.

The Madonna of the Rocks

Dan Brown states that the original commission for the *Madonna of the Rocks* came from the nuns at the chapel of the Immacolata at the church of San Francesco Grande in Milan. It was, in fact, commissioned by monks from that organization. One of the versions of *Madonna of the Rocks* is in the Louvre and this is considered to be entirely Leonardo's work. Experts are not so certain that the other version, at the National Gallery in London, was painted only by him. It has a more "plastic" look to it, which has led to the theory that it was a collaborative effort. This painting not only depicts the Immaculate Conception, but reflects the fact that legends regarding St. John the Baptist were popular in Florence at that time. The painting is of the infant Jesus meeting John the Baptist for the first time. Both children are trying to escape Herod's infamous Massacre of the Innocents and John the Baptist is under the protection of Uriel, the angel. In fact, Leonardo had something of a lifetime obsession with John the Baptist. In the original sketches, Uriel is depicted as being very feminine but in the painting itself the angel has a much more androgynous quality.

The controversy this painting caused was not instigated by the "horror" that its imagery inspired. John the Baptist was Jesus Christ's mentor and there is awkwardness in the Gospels when describing the baptism of Christ by John. John the Baptist was a major figure in Jesus' life. The two boys were cousins, according to the author of the third gospel, St. Luke. As a descendant of Aaron, John could claim the title Priest Messiah. As Jesus is descended from both Aaron and David, he could claim the titles of both Priest Messiah and Royal Messiah. These two cousins, therefore, represented the answers to the Jews' prayers in uniting the spiritual and temporal aspects in the same family. Additionally this situation had occurred during the Maccabean dynasty – Israel's last monarchy. This would not fit in with the Roman Church's "plan" of presenting Jesus as the son of God. He could hardly be so if he looked upon another human being as his teacher.

John the Baptist was a prophet who predicted that a kingly figure would come and fulfill the prophecy that the Roman invaders of Judea would be overthrown. He was considered by the Roman authorities to be so dangerous that he had to be executed. Whether or not this message comes out loud and clear through the painting is debatable. The pose of the children in relation to each other in the second painting is not markedly different to that in the first. The main problem in the composition of the painting relates to the fact that none of the holy characters have haloes in the first painting, and it was for this reason that the monks found it unacceptable, demanding that another version should be made.

There are other differences between the two paintings, such as the second painting being much bluer in color. Uriel's hand, which Dan Brown describes as forming a cutting motion beneath Mary's talon-like hand, no longer points at St. John in the second painting. In the first picture this could have amounted to a prophecy of John's future beheading.

Leonardo had been commissioned to execute the painting on April 25, 1483. He was given the very tight deadline of completing it by the Feast of the Immaculate Conception on December 8. Leonardo, typically, did not meet this deadline, resulting in two lengthy lawsuits. It is possible that Leonardo gave the copy that is now in the Louvre to the King of France, Louis XII, in gratitude for settling the legal problems that arose. This would have necessitated a second copy being painted. The monks had stipulated exactly what they wanted in the picture:

> Item, Our Lady is the center: her mantle shall be of gold brocade and ultramarine blue. Item, her skirt shall be of gold brocade over crimson, in oil, varnished with a fine lacquer...Item, God the Father: his gown shall be of gold brocade and ultramarine blue. Item, the angels shall be gilded and their pleated skirts outlined in oil, in the Greek manner. Item, the mountains and rocks shall be worked in oil, in a colorful manner....

Several changes were made to this, however. We now know that the painting was eventually displayed on August 18, 1508, and the final payment for it was made in October of the same year.

The Mona Lisa

This painting, which must be the most easily recognized in the world, was kept in the Salle des Etats (the Room of States) in the Denon Wing of the Louvre, until 2003. It was then moved to a room that is better able to accommodate the huge crowds that wish to see it. It is reported that it took Leonardo ten years just to paint her lips. It is the only one of his portraits that is indisputably by him although it is neither signed nor dated. It also has more than one name. The

French call the painting *La Joconde* and the Italians call it *La Gioconda*, meaning "a light-hearted woman." It may well have been Leonardo's favorite picture and that could be the reason why he carried it around with him all the time, as Dan Brown says. Another reason could be, however, that it was unfinished.

It was painted in oils on poplar wood and bought originally by the King of France for four thousand ducats. It was transferred to the Louvre after the French Revolution. Napoleon took it and used it to decorate his bedroom until his banishment from France, when it was returned to the Louvre. Originally it was much larger. The two panels that it originally had showed two pillars which revealed that Mona Lisa was sitting on a terrace.

Dan Brown's idea that *Mona Lisa* is an anagram of "AMON L'ISA," thus creating a union of the feminine and masculine is intriguing. However, it could equally be an anagram of "sol (and) anima." This means "sun and soul," and could refer to one of the major religions in the Rome of Constantine the Great, Sol Invictus ("The Invincible Sun") from which many of the Christian traditions were taken. There are several candidates for the identity of the Mona Lisa. Dan Brown's suggestion that it is Leonardo himself in drag could even be true. Computer graphic tests have revealed that there is a close link between the features of the and a self-portrait of Leonardo. However, the painting is widely believed to have been commissioned as a portrait of Madonna Lisa, the wife of Francesco di Bartolomeo del Giocondo.

The reason behind the smile has proven to be just as enigmatic. An Italian doctor has suggested that she was the victim of a disease called "bruxism" which leads to grinding of the teeth while sleeping or at times of stress. Leonardo certainly tried to keep his models as entertained as possible so any stress should have been minimal. He employed six musicians and kept a white Persian cat and a greyhound for company. The style of the smile itself was employed at the time both by Leonardo and other artists, including the master to whom he was apprenticed, Andrea del Verrocchio.

Some people consider the painting to be "boring" but Leonardo was exploring new stylistic territory in the work. One thing that sets the Mona Lisa apart from other portraits of the time is that she is wearing no jewelry. Leonardo also broke the conventions of the time by showing her as too relaxed for a traditionally stiff and formal pose.

The *sfumato style* of painting (which the character Sophie described as "foggy" in *The Da Vinci Code*) in which everything appears as if it were in a mist is one of the main characteristics of Leonardo's paintings. It was his way of expressing "nature experienced." Dan Brown notes that the horizon line of countryside in the painting is uneven and that the left-hand side is lower than the right. According to some, this was Leonardo's way of emphasizing the feminine, darker half of existence. There is a pool of water shown on the right-hand side of the painting, which is higher than the stream which flows on the left. For all we know, there could be a waterfall behind Mona Lisa's head, which feeds water from the pool into the stream. Perhaps nothing more should be read into it than that.

The painting was stolen from the Louvre in 1911 as Dan Brown reports. The thief was an Italian who took it to Italy. It took twenty-four hours before the authorities realized it had been taken, as they assumed that it had been removed by the official museum photographer. It then took a week to search the Louvre, and all that was found was the frame in a stairway. Two years later, the thief, Vincenzo Perugia, offered to sell the painting to the Uffizi Gallery for $100,000, where it was exhibited before being returned to Paris.

In order to steal the picture, Perugia had waited in a small room in the Louvre until it had closed and then walked into the room where the *Mona Lisa* was exhibited. He removed the picture from the wall, and cut it out of the frame. In order to escape from the museum he had to unscrew the doorknob of a door that was supposed to be locked. Perugia had previously been employed by the Louvre to put the paintings under glass, and he therefore had a good knowledge of the layout of the museum.

In 1956 a mentally addled visitor threw acid over the painting and it took several years to restore it. The last time that the painting left the museum was in 1974, when it was exhibited in Japan. As a mark of their gratitude for this, the Japanese presented the Louvre with the thick triplex glass that now covers the painting in its bullet-proof box. It has now been agreed that the painting will never leave the Louvre again – the risks are just too great. It is kept at a constant temperature of 68 degrees Fahrenheit at a humidity level of 55 per cent. It has a built-in air conditioner and nine pounds of silica gel ensure there is no change in the air condition. The box is opened once a year to check the painting and service the air conditioning system. Nobody has dared to clean the painting for fear of damaging it, and the colors of the paint beneath the dirt may be far more brilliant than we can see now.

The Last Supper

Duke Ludovico commissioned Leonardo to paint *The Last Supper* on the refectory wall of his family chapel and burial place, the Santa Maria della Grazie in Milan. It measures 30 feet by 14 feet, and the work was finished in 1498 after three years of labor. Breaking with convention, Leonardo seats all the apostles on the same side of the table, in groups of three, making them appear like small focus groups. The characters all appear larger than they are, as the table is too small to accommodate them comfortably. Christ is made the focal point by placing three windows behind him, the largest of which frames the upper part of his head and body. He is shown as being in a state of absolute calm while the apostles around him are clearly agitated.

Leonardo had the greatest trouble finding a person with a suitable head to portray Judas. Apparently it took him over a year to find a face of appropriate evil. As a last resort he said that he would use the face of the prior of Santa Maria della

Grazie as a model: "Until now I held off holding him up to ridicule in his own monastery." He never asked permission to use the faces of people in his paintings and they were not aware that he had done so. Judas is the only figure in the painting that is not leaning in towards Christ, and his hand is hovering over a dish, illustrating Christ's words in the Gospels: "He that dippeth his hand with me into the dish, he shall betray me."

The painting was extremely popular from the start. The King of France was so enthusiastic about it that he wanted the whole wall to be taken down and shipped to France, but the logistical problems were too great and it has therefore remained where it was originally painted.

Sadly, it is now in a bad state of repair. Part of the reason for this is that the chromatic colors which were used were unsuitable for painting onto a wall. It deteriorated quite rapidly, and in 1652, a door was actually cut through the center! The effects of this can still be seen.

The Napoleonic troops took over the refectory as a stable in 1796 and although Napoleon forbade any damage to the painting, the troops threw clay at the apostles. The room was then used to store hay and just to show that things could get even worse, a flood in 1800 caused the painting to be covered in a green mould.

However, robust to the last, the painting went on to survive an allied attack on the church in 1943 which destroyed the refectory roof. The painting was protected by sandbags, but it was badly damaged. An entire restoration with the most painstaking detail was then carried out and completed in 1954. Very little of the original paint exists, and it has been impossible to recreate the original expression on the faces of the apostles, although the outlines of the figures were visible during restoration.

Despite the sustained devastation throughout the centuries, it appears that the person on Christ's right hand side is a woman. As Dan Brown said in his interview with ABC News' *Primetime Monday* host Elizabeth Vargas:

> *Paintings are symbolic by nature. The idea of the "V" in the painting, the "V" being the symbol, long before Leonardo da Vinci, the symbol of the feminine. The symbol here is essentially the womb, in its very strict, symbolic sense.*

In addition to forming this "V" symbol, the mirror images of the Magdalene and Christ can be seen to form the letter "M" for "Magdalene." This is seen more clearly in the copy of the painting by an unknown sixteenth century artist, kept at the Museo da Vinci at Tongerlo in Belgium. However, Bruce Bucher in his article "Does 'The Da Vinci Code' Crack Leonardo?" (*New York Times*, August 3, 2003) disagrees. He points out that in other contemporary Florentine depictions of the Last Supper, not only was the betrayal emphasized more than the Eucharist and the chalice, but, "St. John was invariably represented as a beautiful young man whose special affinity with Jesus was expressed by sitting at Jesus' right."

The Adoration of the Magi
Leonardo was commissioned in 1480 to paint this work for the monastery of San Donato a Scopeto, near Florence. Leonardo was to be paid through a complicated land deal, in which there was a penalty clause that stipulated that he would lose everything if he failed to deliver the painting on time. As ever with commissioned works, Leonardo was unable to fulfill this obligation.

The painting represents the Three Wise Men visiting the newborn Christ and his mother Mary. Among the large crowd of sixty-six people and eleven animals, there is a shepherd boy standing alone on the extreme right of the painting and this figure is thought to be a portrait of the young Leonardo. The ruins in the background represent the decline of Paganism. This symbolism is typical of that time. However, on closer inspection of the painting using infrared light, it was found that there were figures constructing a staircase, representing, according to some, the Renaissance.

As the painting was unfinished, it was possible to see the sketching underneath the ochre paint and therefore to reveal how Leonardo worked. *The Adoration* had always been considered to be one of Italy's most important paintings. That is until Maurizio Seracini came along. He is an eminent art diagnostician, who has spent nearly thirty years examining works of art. He was asked by the Uffizi Gallery to assess whether *Adoration of the Magi* was too fragile to be restored. He then announced to a startled world through *New York Times* reporter Melinda Henneberger on April 21, 2002, that results of his extensive test revealed "None of the paint we see on the *Adoration* today was put there by Leonardo. God knows who did, but it was not Leonardo. The guy was not even a very good artist." Some thought that he was simply trying to cause a sensation. As Dan Brown writes in *The Da Vinci Code*, Seracini maintains that the grey-green lines were drawn by Leonardo and was highly indignant that Leonardo could ever have been held responsible for some of the lines painted in brown. He stated that the Madonna's right foot, for example, has pointed toes and heel, the baby's little foot looks as if it were carved out of wood, and the child's hair looked like a "baby toupee." Seracini felt that Leonardo, with his detailed knowledge of anatomy, had been insulted over the centuries with the belief that this was considered to be his work entirely.

His theory has been backed up by one of the world's leading Leonardo scholars, Carlo Pedretti of the University of California at Los Angeles. He has known Seracini for 30 years, and says there is no doubt that the results of his recent tests are correct. "From what he showed me," Pedretti says, "it's clear that Leonardo's original sketch was gone over by an anonymous painter."

The Shroud of Turin
One of the most fascinating theories regarding Leonardo involves the Shroud of Turin, which is alleged to be the image of Christ imprinted on the shroud that covered him after his death. It is an odd fact that Leonardo never painted the Crucifixion, which was one of the major artistic themes

of the time, and some believe that the Shroud of Turin was created by him as his own idiosyncratic interpretation of it. The Catholic Church allowed scientists access to the Shroud for extensive investigation for only a single period of five days and five nights in 1978. The cloth itself has been carbon dated and found to have been made between 1260 and 1390, with 95% certainty. The Church announced this, probably much to their embarrassment, on October 13, 1988. One of the arguments against Leonardo having created it is that this was a considerable time before Leonardo was born in 1452. However, cloth from that earlier period was widely available in Leonardo's time, as it had been brought back to Europe during the Crusades. It is possible that Leonardo would have used this material if he wanted to convince others that it was Christ's shroud. It is impossible to say when the image itself was placed on the cloth, as carbon dating will not reveal this.

The face on the shroud seems to closely resemble that of Leonardo in his self-portrait. As discussed previously, Leonardo also appears to be the model of the Mona Lisa. Similar to Alfred Hitchcock, he seemed to enjoy playing cameo roles in his works. There is no doubt that he had the skills to produce a work such as the Shroud of Turin and to disguise how it was achieved.

For 500 years the Shroud of Turin belonged to the royal family of Italy, the Savoys. The remaining heir to the family donated it to the Catholic Church in 1983. Also in the palace of the Savoys in Turin is the only known self-portrait of Leonardo. It is likely that the Shroud would have been commissioned by either the Duke of Savoy or the Pope, or possibly both of them in league. The theory is that they wanted a substitute of the existing Shroud of Lirey made. The Shroud of Lirey was first exhibited in 1389, and was denounced as false by the local bishop of Troyes, who declared it "cunningly painted, the truth being attested by the artist who painted it." This could obviously not apply to the Shroud of Turin, which to this day we are unable to ascertain how it was created. We do know that Leonardo experimented constantly with new painting techniques. For example an x-ray of his painting *John the Baptist* reveals no brush stokes and appears to be painted like a mist. No painter has managed to replicate this skill.

In 1976 a photograph of the Shroud was put through a V-8 Image Analyzer, and it was discovered that three-dimensional information was encoded into it. It revealed a perfect relief of a human form, which would be impossible to create through painting. In fact, the modification of the fibers that create the image suggests some sort of burning process has taken place. This could have been achieved through a bas-relief made in an oven, and then the image would have been burned onto the cloth. It was common in the Middle Ages for bas-reliefs of the dead to be made and put on the top of graves. Leonardo certainly had the knowledge to do this and had received training in sculpture.

There is also the convincing argument that the Shroud was created using a camera obscura which is a darkened box with either a convex lens or an aperture. The image of an external object is projected onto a screen inside the box. There are drawings of such a camera by Leonardo. He was familiar with the necessary chemicals, such as silver nitrate, that would be necessary to achieve this and he studied optics. This theory also explains why the back side of the body of the shroud appears taller than the front side. It takes only a slight difference in distance between the subject and the camera to make such a difference in size.

This whole issue, together with the fact that generations of pilgrims have worshipped the Shroud as being the image of Christ, not knowing that it was possibly Leonardo's own image, would have amused him greatly. The Shroud is perhaps the greatest riddle that we have inherited from him.

Leonardo was close to King Francis I – in fact so much so that there is a painting of Leonardo dying in his arms. Francis was a Savoy who married into the Medici family and therefore Leonardo was as well connected as it was possible to be.

Leonardo would be the obvious choice for someone to create such a work as the Shroud of Turin. There was also the advantage of Leonardo's unconventional attitude to religion. He would have had no fears of eternal damnation for the blasphemy of the act. As a scientist and homosexual, he was already beyond redemption in the eyes of the Catholic Church. He saw no reason why he should not work on Sundays. He never once mentioned God in the 13,000 pages of the notes that he wrote. In particular he despised the flourishing relic trade in which merchants made fortunes selling supposedly holy objects to the gullible. He was charismatic, handsome, amusing and popular. In his repertoire of humor was included what he referred to as "Pope Frightening." An example of this was when he once told the Pope, probably Leo X, Giovanni de Medici, that he had a dragon in a small box. When he had worked the Pope up to a sufficient level of terror, he opened the box and out jumped a small lizard, painted silver, with wings attached to its back. In short, the hoax of the Shroud of Turin would have appealed to his deep enjoyment of the sacrilegious.

The nails in the palms on the Shroud are positioned precisely where they should be if it truly represented a person who had been crucified. People were always crucified in this way, since nails driven at other points through the hands (as the Crucifixion of Christ has always been depicted) would not have been able to support a human body upon a cross. Assuming the Shroud is a fake, its creator would have had a precise knowledge of the crucifixion process. It is probable that Leonardo crucified some of the corpses that he had at his disposal and there is evidence that he studied the process.

Chapter Two
The Priory of Sion, its Grand Masters and the Plantards

IN *THE DA VINCI CODE*, ROBERT LANGDON INTERPRETS THE INITIALS "P.S." ETCHED ON SOPHIE NEVEU'S SAFE DEPOSIT KEY, AS INDICATING THE PRIORY OF SION. THIS ABBREVIATION ALSO APPEARS ON ONE OF THE DOCUMENTS THAT BÉRENGER SAUNIÈRE, WHOM WE SHALL LEARN OF IN CHAPTER FOUR, FOUND INSIDE THE CHURCH AT RENNES-LE-CHÂTEAU AND APPEARED ON THE TOMBSTONE OF MARIE DE BLANCHEFORT WHICH WAS ONCE IN THE CHURCH GRAVEYARD.

The subject of the Priory of Sion is the basic undercurrent running throughout the plot of *The DaVinci Code*. Although unaware of its existence before she met Langdon, every aspect of Sophie's life had been dominated by it. This puts her in precisely the same situation as many readers, who, while raised Christian, were unaware of the real historical forces at work behind Christianity. Ann Evans, the researcher that Michael Baigent, Richard Leigh and Henry Lincoln employed while writing their book about the Priory, *The Messianic Legacy*, had thirty-five years of experience in the field and yet she stated that she had never before encountered so many obstacles and contradictions while conducting research. The uncertainty of the so-called "evidence" creates a nebulous atmosphere which makes the Priory all the more intriguing. And the truth which is known is decidedly murky.

From the Beginning
Most of the actual "evidence" of the existence of the Priory has been deposited in the Bibliothèque Nationale in Paris, which, say many researchers, has made obtaining the relevant documents quite difficult. Such claims tend to indicate

that at least certain administrators at the French national library are in league with the Priory of Sion, which since the 1950s has enjoyed leaving tantalizing tidbits of information there for researchers to stumble across.

There are two documents that were of particular interest to Baigent, Leigh and Lincoln when they were writing their authoritative 1982 book *Holy Blood, Holy Grail*, concerning the Merovingian bloodline. The first is the enigmatic Dossiers Secrets, a collection of seemingly unconnected papers which were mysteriously added to and taken from periodically. The second is a work known as *Le Serpent Rouge* (*The Red Snake*), perhaps written by Jean Cocteau, as it echoes his style. It contains a genealogy of the Merovingians, a ground plan of l'Église de Saint-Sulpice and thirteen poems relating to the signs of the zodiac (including a thirteenth sign inserted between Scorpio and Sagittarius: Ophiuchus, "the Serpent Holder"). The attributed authors of both of these documents (four men in all) have died in unexplained circumstances.

The Priory of Sion, or the "Prieuré de Sion" as it is known in French, is said to have its ultimate roots in a Hermetic or Gnostic society led by an Egyptian sage named Ormus in about 46 AD. "Ormus" is also the subtitle that the Priory of Sion adopted in 1188 when it changed its name from "Order of Sion." At this time they also referred to themselves as the "Ordre de la Rose-Croix Veritas" ("Order of the True Rose-Cross"), indicating that the Priory of Sion may have in fact been the original Rosicrucian order.

Not until the Middle Ages does an organization relating to Sion become known to historians. The Abbey of Orval in Stenay (once called "Satanicum"), located in the Ardennes in northern France, was founded by a group of monks from Calabria in Italy in 1070, led by the Merovingian "Prince Ursus" (rumored to be Dagobert II's great-grandson, Sigisbert VI). These monks formed the basis of the Order of Sion into which they were absorbed, along with Godfroi de Bouillon's Templar Order in 1099 – the year that he captured Jerusalem. Godfroi de Bouillon was not only the Duke of Lorraine. As a descendant of Dagobert II, he was, as a Merovingian, a rightful King (see Chapter Three for a full discussion). Stenay was one of the two capital cities of the Merovingians. It was in the nearby sacred Forest of Woëvres that King Dagobert II was assassinated while hunting on December 23, 679, as Dan Brown states, stabbed in the eye while sleeping under a tree. It is thought that his godson had assassinated him under the orders of Pepin the Fat, the turncoat Mayor of Dagobert's palace.

It appears that the remit of the Priory of Sion has always been the restoration of the Merovingian dynasty and bloodline to the thrones of Europe, having lost their birthright after Dagobert's assassination. Through various political pacts and marriages, the line eventually came to include various noble and royal houses, such as the Blanchefort, Gisors, Saint-Clair, Montesquieu, Montpézat, Poher, Luisignan, Plantard and Habsburg-Lorraine families. It is confirmed by records of the time that the headquarters of the Order were the Abbey of Nôtre Dame du Mont de Sion, which lies to the south of Jerusalem. It was well-fortified and built on the ruins of a Byzantine basilica. According to a 1990 issue of *Biblical Archaeology* magazine, Mt. Sion seems to have been the headquarters of the Ebionites of Jerusalem. These followers of Jesus considered his brother James, and not the Apostle Paul, to be the rightful leader of the Christian church.

What is perhaps not so certain is the claim that the Priory of Sion, as Langdon puts it, "has a well-documented history of reverence for the sacred feminine," and reveres Mary Magdalene, whom they hold to be Christ's wife, as an embodiment of that feminine principle. As Tracy Twyman of *Dagobert's Revenge* magazine writes:

> Mary Magdalene is held up by many Grail researchers as some
> feminist heroine and they claim that she was "written out of the
> Bible" because the Church was threatened by her femininity. But
> neither Magdalene nor the Church fathers thought in such lan-
> guage, nor would they even have conceived of such a notion.
> Magdalene was a threat to the Church not because she was a

woman, but because she was the mother of Christ's children — the heirs to his royal and priestly lineage. By all rights they should have been the proper inheritors not only of Christ's church, but of his royal throne in Jerusalem (which in the eyes of some should have also held hegemony over the entire world). Both of these claims were a threat to the Church, which not only wished to rule the world spiritually, but secularly as well, for the Church proclaimed that it had the right to make kings, regardless of their birthright.

Godfroi de Bouillon was well aware that he was a member of a Grail family, and therefore a Merovingian and de facto King of Jerusalem who could trace his family origins back through the Davidic line. After capturing Jerusalem, he founded the Templars. Even though there were three other Christian armies bound for Palestine, Godfroi seemed to know that he would be chosen to be the King of Jerusalem. He had, after all, sold everything before leaving, and made clear that his intention was to stay in Jerusalem for life. However, he refused the title of "King," and accepted only that of "Defender of the Holy Sepulchre." Baigent, Leigh and Lincoln put forward the idea that the aforementioned group of Calabrian monks, which disappeared without explanation from Orval, is the same group of non-militant advisers who are known to have accompanied Godfroi to Jerusalem. They also suggest that it was this very group of people who selected the King of Jerusalem.

The Order of Sion appears to have been based in the Abbey of Nôtre Dame du Mont de Sion from the public foundation of the Templars in 1118 until 1152. The Templars were recognized as a religious-military order in 1127 at Troyes by the court of the Count of Champagne and Hugues de Payen was selected as the Grand Master.

When Louis VII of France returned from the second crusade he brought back ninety-five members of the order. Seven of them entered the military force of the Knights Templar and the rest re-established their French connection in Orleans. The documents with which Louis VII established the order in France are still in existence.

The Abbey of Orval became a house for the Cistercian order in 1131. This order had been seriously impoverished in the past, but their circumstances improved along with those of the Templars. Both acquired huge wealth and areas of land.

The name of the Ordre de Sion has appeared on documents from at least July 19, 1116. A further charter dated 1178 was found, bearing the seal of Pope Alexander III and confirming the Order's land holdings not only in the Holy Land, but throughout continental Europe.

In 1956 the Copper Scroll from Qumran was deciphered at Manchester University. This revealed that the Ark of the Covenant and an enormous treasure of gold bullion had been buried under the Temple of Solomon. In 1979, Pierre Plantard de Saint-Clair, the last known Grand Master of the Priory of Sion, told Baigent, Leigh and Lincoln that the Priory of Sion possessed the treasure from the Temple of Jerusalem, which had been plundered by the Romans during the revolt of 66 AD. The scene is depicted on the Arch of Titus in Rome. When the Visigoths later plundered Rome, the treasure was taken, perhaps to the south of France, near Rennes-le-Château. M. Plantard went on to say that the "treasure" would be returned to Israel when the "time was right." He did not specify whether this is treasure in the traditional sense or a collection of documents, or – as Dan Brown suggests – a map to indicate the hiding place of the Holy Grail.

There is also a legend stating that the Cathar "heretics" were in possession of this treasure. The Cathars (or "Albigensians") were headquartered in the Languedoc area of what is now southern France, where Rennes-le-Château is situated. In 1209 they were subjected to a massacre, the scale of which amounted to ethnic cleansing at the hands of 30,000 soldiers. Languedoc was a center of great learning at the time – at the expense of Roman Catholicism. It was the Cathars' casual attitude to religion in general, and their lack of respect of Roman Catholicism in particular, that was more responsible than anything for the hatred they spawned within the ecclesiastical authorities. Among the many "transgressions" of which they were accused, it is thought that they practiced birth control and abortion. The treasure that was reputedly in their keeping was thought to transcend that of "mere" gold, and could have been either the Grail chalice itself or knowledge that would bring about unimaginable riches.

The Rise and Fall of the Knights Templar

The reason for the existence of the Templars was ostensibly to protect the roads to Jerusalem for the pilgrims journeying there. However, as Robert Langdon tells Sophie in *The Da Vinci Code*, their real mission was to investigate what was hidden beneath the foundations of the Temple of Solomon, which not coincidentally, was the location of the Templars' living quarters in Jerusalem.

The Templars were the heroes of their time. The sons of noble families joined in droves. They became political advisers to monarchs at the highest level, and everyone wanted to bask in their reflected glory. They wallowed in generous donations and their influence grew enormously. They owned their own seaports and founded hospitals. Their fleet was the first to use a magnetic compass. Ironically, every member had to sign over all his possessions to the order and take a vow of poverty. They had to cut their hair, but were not allowed to cut their beards. They were not allowed to retreat in battle, and were obliged to fight to the death. Pope Innocent II issued a Papal Bull in 1139 which stated that they were totally independent of any authority and were, effectively, a law unto themselves.

It was the Templars who founded the first international banking system. They built the most graceful and elegant Gothic cathedrals of Europe, such as Nôtre Dame in Paris, at this time. The word "Gothic," in fact, has no connection to the Goths, but derives from the Greek *goetic* which means "magical (action)." This reflects the sacred geometry that Templar stonemasons used to build these cathedrals.

By 1306, the Knights Templars' wealth had grown to such an extent that the King of France, Philippe IV (also known as Philippe the Fair), became decidedly nervous. He owed them a large amount of money and was painfully aware that their influence from every point of view was greater than his own. He was restricted from taxing the clergy through a Vatican edict. This did not put Philippe off however and he had the Pope, Boniface VIII, caught and murdered. The next pope, Benedict XI, fared no better – he died suspiciously soon afterwards. At last Philippe's favored candidate, Bertrand of Goth, became Pope Clement V. Then Philippe went to work against the Knights Templar, leveling charges of heresy, to which they were particularly vulnerable. The Knights Templar refused to share the accepted Christian views of the Crucifixion and their business activities necessitated them mixing with Jews, Gnostics and Muslims, including a secret relationship with the notorious Muslim equivalent to the Templars – the Hashashin or Assassins. They were also said to worship a devil named Baphomet, the bearded male head that Langdon speaks of, which supposedly spoke to the Templars and gave them magical powers.

Philippe's plan was carried out on arguably the original "Friday the 13th": Friday, October 13, 1307. Since then, Friday the 13th has always been considered to be a bad day in Western culture. Philippe had issued orders to his governors throughout France, which were opened by his seneschals at precisely the same time. All Templars were to be arrested, their preceptories taken over, and their goods confiscated. After imprisonment, interrogation and torture, they were burned at the stake. Witnesses testified that the Knights Templar were guilty of a variety of crimes, including necromancy, homosexuality, defiling the image of Christ and witchcraft. However, despite these extreme measures, Philippe did not achieve his objective of securing for himself the treasure of the Knights Templar.

Perhaps the attack was not such a surprise. Just before the massacre a new contingent of Knights Templar troops was sent from Rossillon in the Spanish province of Aragon to Rennes-le-Château in southern France, where they established a stronghold on the mountain called Bézu. Out of all the Knights Templar, it was only they who were not targeted.

This may be because Pope Clement V (a.k.a. "Bertrand de Goth") was the son of Ida de Blanchefort, from the same family as a former Templar Grand Master, Bertrand de Blanchefort. It seems more than likely that these family connections saved the skins of this Templar contingent on the day the arrests took place.

In all probability, the Grand Master of the Knights Templar at that time, Jacques de Molay, was also aware of what was coming, as he arranged for the treasure to be shipped out of France. It is said that most of the ships went to Scotland, but Philippe knew nothing of this. He continued his persecution by trying to persuade other European monarchs to hunt down the Templars in their own countries. He arranged for Clement V to outlaw the Knights Templar in 1312. Eventually Jacques de Molay was burned at the stake in 1314. As a parting gesture, he prayed out loud through the torture of the flames that his persecutors, Pope Clement and Philippe, would join him in death within a year and explain their deeds to God's court. It seemed to work. Pope Clement died within a month and King Philippe died under mysterious circumstances within the year. Their deaths were possibly caused by poison, which the Templars were adept at using.

Edward II of England was in an awkward position. He was the son-in-law of Philippe, but he did not share Philippe's obsessive loathing of the Templars and had no desire to persecute them. Against his better judgment he implemented the Inquisition and had a large number of Templars arrested. However, they were given comparatively light sentences and were not subjected to the continued persecution that Philippe meted out to the Templars in France.

In Scotland, the Papal Bull was disdainfully ignored and the Templars flourished. Each Bruce and Stewart King from the time of Robert the Bruce has been a Knight Templar from birth, so there wasn't much chance of Philippe's orders being carried out there.

The Cutting of the Elm

The Order of the Temple (Knights Templar) and the Priory of Sion shared the same Grand Master and were two arms of the same organization until something called the "cutting of the elm," which took place at Gisors in 1188. This falling out between the two orders was supposedly caused by the so-called "treason" of Grand Master Gérard de Ridefort, which according to the Dossiers Secrets, resulted in Europe's loss of Jerusalem to the Saracens.

There is an historic record of the "cutting of the elm" at Gisors in 1188, although no source except for the "Priory Documents" connects this event to the Templars or to the Priory of Sion. It is one of those apparently silly, medieval tales which one suspects hides a greater and more solemn truth. There was, in fact, an elm in the Champ Sacré – the sacred field which had been deemed as such for centuries. The tree was said to have been over eight hundred years old and so large that nine men could hardly link hands around its circumference. The field was used for meetings between the kings of England and France.

According to one account, matters reached boiling point on one occasion between Henry II of England and Philippe II of France. In an example, perhaps, of the eternal antipathy that exists between the English and the French, Henry II and his entourage took refuge from the Sun that was beating down on the field, leaving the French victims to the unremitting heat. Unable to bear it any more and possibly humiliated by the jibes of the English, the numerically superior French attacked the English, who retreated into the city of Gisors. In an act of belligerent defiance, Philippe II had the tree cut down and returned to Paris in a vile temper, saying that he would never again play the part of woodcutter.

Another account says that Philippe told Henry that he intended to cut down the tree. Henry was enraged by this and put hoops of iron around the tree trunk to reinforce it. The French attacked and Henry's son, Richard the

Lionhearted, and his men protected the tree, but with great losses. The French won and the tree was cut down
.

Both of these accounts are probably allegorical tales pointing at something altogether different than what is apparent. However, it does seem that at this point in history the Order of Sion and the Knights Templar parted company. The Order was to continue its dedication to the Merovingian line and was known as the Priory of Sion from this time foreword, while the Knights Templar appear to have allied themselves with the Scottish royal bloodline, the House of Stuart, an offshoot of the Merovingian house. The Stuarts later, when exiled in France, became deeply involved in Freemasonry and founded what is known as the "Scottish Rite," which has more degrees than other Masonic organizations and promises knowledge of mysteries that are essentially Scottish.

There are records deposited in Orleans which suggest that members of the Priory of Sion misbehaved there, angering both the Pope and the King of France, Louis XIV, with various decadent practices. By 1619 the authorities lost patience and the Priory of Sion was forced to leave their premises at Saint-Samson in Orleans. It seems unlikely that this was of any great importance in the total history of the Priory of Sion. Rather, it suggests that Orleans by that time was an outpost of little consequence and the main thrust of the Priory's activities was being conducted elsewhere.

One thing that in turn annoyed the Priory of Sion about Louis XIV was his decision to give France a new national Meridian, as calculated by the astronomer Cassini, to pass through the Paris Observatory. Dan Brown mentions that the "Rose Line" (supposedly the original, ancient meridian) runs through l'Église de Saint-Sulpice. *Le Serpent Rouge* and other "Priory documents" maintain that this older meridian on the north-south axis ran through several hermetic churches in France, including Saint-Sulpice in Paris, the Lady of the Roses cathedral in Rodez, St. Vincent's in Carcasonne and the Church of St. Stephen's in Bourges. Significantly, it also ran through Rennes-le-Château, whose name itself comes from Rhédae, the name of one of the Celtic tribes that considered the Rose Line sacred. Louis XIV replaced romanticism and religious significance with a mundane line with the intention of facilitating commercial life.[2]

The Nostradamus Connection

In the sixteenth century, the Lorraine and Guise families made repeated attempts to take over the French throne, which was at that time in the hands of the Valois family. Their efforts, as *Holy Blood, Holy Grail* hints, were coordinated by the Priory of Sion. François de Guise was on the point of achieving this in 1563 when he was assassinated. This did not deter them however, and by the end of the century the Valois family disappeared. The Guise family also suffered considerably from the feud and they were no longer able to realize their ambition.

One of those suspected of helping the Guise and Lorraine houses is Nostradamus. As he was astrologer to the French court, ideally positioned to advise the two families on matters of state that concerned them, he could have acted as a spy on their behalf. It is also thought that many of Nostradamus' writings are not the prophecies that they are generally considered to be, but codes of various kinds revealing the secret plans of the Priory of Sion.

Some of Nostradamus' "prophecies" referred not to the future, but to the contemporary past and present and specifically to the Merovingians and the Knights Templar. According to Gérard de Sède, who wrote extensively on the Cathars, the Templars, the Merovingian dynasty, Saunière and Rennes-le-Château, Nostradamus spent time in Lorraine. He is said to have been shown a mysterious book upon which he later based his writings. This book was kept at the Abbey of Orval which, as we have seen, was the place where the Priory probably originated.

[2] It has been pointed out that the meridian line in Washington, D.C. was also moved when Greenwich in England became the International Meridian. Capital Street is Washington's present meridian line on the North-South axis. Until it was changed, the "zero meridian" line was on 16th Street, on which you will find a Scottish Rite Temple and other esoteric churches and monuments.

The same families have been consistently involved in the religious disturbances of the sixteenth century, the French civil war known as the Fronde of the seventeenth century and the Masonic conspiracies of the eighteenth century. They have also featured prominently in the history of the Priory of Sion. They owe their heritage to the Merovingian line, which passed through Dagobert II and his son Sigisbert II.

The Grand Masters of the Priory of Sion

The list of Grand Masters that Dan Brown provides in *The Da Vinci Code* appeared originally in the *Dossiers Secrets*. The list consists partly of those who one would expect to be involved in a clandestine organization. Many of them had connections with such places as Rennes-le-Château and Stenay and many were also connected in various ways to the influential Lorraine family.

On the other hand, there are individuals who are well-known in other contexts, but apparently incongruous in this one. One thing that they all had in common were their unorthodox religious beliefs. Baigent, Leigh, and Lincoln have concluded that the title of Grand Master of the Priory has been passed down through families of Merovingian descent, but if there is nobody available through these means for some reason, an outsider is invited to take over the position. This would explain how Leonardo da Vinci, Isaac Newton and Jean Cocteau were listed.

One curious "coincidence" concerns Cocteau. After the "cutting of the elm" in 1188, the first Grand Master of the Priory of Sion was Jean de Gisors. Since that time, every male Grand Master has adopted the name "Jean" and each of the four females who took on the role became "Jeanne." However Jean de Gisors was listed in the Priory documents not as "Jean I" but as "Jean II" bringing about speculation that Jean I was either John the Baptist, John the Evangelist (John the Beloved of the Fourth Gospel) or St. John the Divine, the author of The Book of Revelation. John the Baptist was the prophet who predicted the arrival of the Messiah, a royal figure who would defeat the Roman invaders. John the Baptist presented a great danger to Herod-Antipas of Galilee who had him executed later. Jesus Christ was, in fact, a disciple of John the Baptist. Christian scholars have always found it difficult to explain why Jesus Christ should appear subordinate to John the Baptist and some heretics throughout the years have even proclaimed that it was John, not Jesus, who was the Christ. These people are known as "Johannites."

Jean Cocteau, according to the Dossiers Secrets, was Jean XXIII, as he was the twenty-third male to hold the position. When Pope Pius XII died in 1959, Jean Cocteau was still the Grand Master. The new pope, Cardinal Angelo Giuseppe Rancalli, caused considerable consternation when he chose his papal name to be John XXIII. This was the same name taken by the infamous "antipope," who set himself up as a rival to the papacy in the fifteenth century. It was inexplicable that the new pope would want to adopt this name.

In 1976, a collection of poems was published which were said to have been written by Pope John XXIII. It is not certain that they were really penned by him, but the introduction throws an interesting spanner in the works. It suggests that John XXIII was a member of the "Rose-Croix." As we have seen, the subtitle that the Priory of Sion adopted in 1188 was "Rose-Croix Veritas." Does this mean that Pope John XXIII was a member of the Priory of Sion? It certainly seems beyond coincidence that the election of John XXIII of the Priory of Sion would coincide with that of a pope who chose, against everyone's wishes, to call himself John XXIII. It is impossible that the list was contrived since it was deposited in the Bibliothèque Nationale in 1956 and the Pope was not in power until 1958.

Pope John XXIII went on to bring about the greatest changes to the Roman Catholic church that had ever been seen. He reversed the church's position on Freemasonry; for two hundred years previous, Catholics had been forbidden from joining. Now that sanction was lifted. In his apostolic letter of June 1960, he attached particular significance to "The Precious Blood of Jesus." He said that what had actually redeemed man was Christ's suffering and the shedding of his blood. These two aspects of Jesus' story thereby extended to assume greater significance than either the Resurrection or the Crucifixion itself. It has been said that it changes the whole basis that supports Christian belief. In other words, it was not necessary for Jesus to die for the purpose of redeeming man's sins. This effectively rendered the Crucifixion and the Resurrection as irrelevant.

Some of the Alleged Grand Masters

Nicolas Flamel *born circa 1330, probably in Pontoise, France, died circa 1418, Paris*
Nicolas Flamel was the first Grand Master of the Priory not to have a family connection with the other Grand Masters. His name is perhaps familiar to aficionados of Harry Potter. It was Flamel who was said to have worked with the headmaster of Hogwarts School of Witchcraft and Wizardry, Professor Albus Dumbledore, on alchemical matters such the changing of lead into gold. His posthumous fame comes from his life-time interest in the magical arts and some people are certain that he never died! In *Harry Potter and the Philosopher's Stone* he was said to be about 665 years old. This would more or less make sense as he was actually born in 1330. He was a copyist of illuminated texts and a bookseller in Paris. Flamel educated himself through the books that passed through his hands. It is said that one night, Flamel had a dream in which an angel appeared to him, showing him a book which seemed to consist of pages made of thin wood and a cover of well-fashioned copper. He was unable to take the book from the angel as he awoke from the dream.

However, that was not the last of the matter and so began a phase of his life that would change everything for him.

Some time later a visitor came to his bookstall, desperately in need of money. He offered to sell him a book. Flamel was able to identify some of the characters on the copper cover as Greek and the pages seemed to be made from the wood of tree saplings instead of the more usual parchment. Flamel bought the book immediately recognizing its similarity to that he had seen in his dream. He could make out that the book had the rather snappy title of *The Sacred Book of Abraham the Jew, Prince, Priest, Levite, Astrologer and Philosopher to that Tribe of Jews who by the Wrath of God were Dispersed amongst the Gauls.*

At that time there were no Jews in France as they had all been driven out. Flamel realized that only a Jewish scholar would be able to help him translate the book so he copied out a few pages and set off for neighboring Spain in 1382. At first he had no luck as all the Jews that he met were suspicious of him. He was about to head back home to France when he happened to meet a converted Jew by the name of Maestro Canches who lived in Leon. Canches was initially suspicious of him too, until Flamel mentioned that the book was by Abraham the Jew who was well-known to him. He was able to translate the few pages that Flamel had brought with him, but was unable to return to France to translate the rest because of the persecution and the fact that he was too old to travel. However, as a result of the pages that Flamel could now understand, it is reported that he conducted the first successful alchemical transmutation at noon on January 17. Soon thereafter he became spectacularly wealthy and devoted much of this wealth to the foundation of charitable organizations such as hospitals and churches.

René d'Anjou born Jan. 16, 1409, *Angers, France*, died July 10, 1480, *Aix-en-Provence*
René d'Anjou was also known as "Good King René." Among his many titles, he was nominally King of Jerusalem. He lived a colorful life and although he was one of the first to codify the rules of chivalry, the "Good King's" sense of values was at times at odds with what we would consider honorable behavior. He was taken prisoner at Bulgnéville in 1431, and handed over to Philip the Good, Duke of Burgundy, but was released on parole in 1432, after giving his sons John and Louis as hostage.

He became Grand Master at the age of ten, which according to the *Dossiers Secrets* was not unusual. He was later admitted to several other orders including the Order of the Crescent, which for some reason displeased the Pope. René used the Cross of Lorraine as his own personal device which symbolized his royal house. The Cross was later used by the Free French Forces in World War II under Charles de Gaulle. It was also used by Godfroi de Bouillon and the Knights Templar.

René had a great influence on the advent of the Renaissance and one of his daughters married Henry VI of England. He also apparently had some kind of liaison with Joan of Arc whose mission was to save France from the English. René is said to have been with her when she went to the Dauphin's court at Chinon and was possibly by her side at the siege of Orleans. Her sudden success in achieving her aim of ensuring that the weak Dauphin would become King was, it seems, largely due to the influence of Iolande d'Anjou, the mother of René. Many feel that the situation was manipulated and that there was a secret organization operating behind the scenes – the Priory, obviously.

René was a poet, and illustrated his own literature. He had a deep interest in esoteric and mystical matters. Although many paintings have been attributed to him, some of them may not actually be his. They bear his arms, but may have been done by court painters. He had a great influence on the Medici family of Florence who were responsible for many significant works of the Renaissance. The classics were translated at this time and Greek was taught at the University of Florence for the first time in centuries. The first public library in Europe, the San Marco Library, was founded in 1444 in Florence. René introduced the theme of Arcadia, the Greek pastoral paradise which signified for the Priory the "Golden Age" that they believed would occur once the Merovingians were returned to their thrones. The concept of an "underground stream" became something of a fixation to René, symbolizing the "subterranean" movement among occultists to hasten the coming of the new Arcadia. These ideas spread quickly throughout Europe via the art and literature of the time.

Sandro Filipepi born 1445, Florence (Italy), died May 17, 1510, Florence
Born in 1444, he is better known as the painter Botticelli, who was a great influence on Pre-Raphaelite painters of the nineteenth century. He is the second on the Priory of Sion list not to have a blood connection with the families whose genealogies are detailed in the *Dossiers Secrets*, but he was well-connected to some of these royal houses. Among his illustrious patrons were the Medicis. As testimony to his interest in the esoteric, the design of one of the first Tarot packs is ascribed to either him or his tutor, Mantegna. His paintings *Primavera* (Spring) and *The Birth of Venus* are based on the dream-like concepts of Arcadia and the underground stream.

Robert Boyle born January 25, 1627, Lismore Castle, County Waterford, Ireland, died December 31, 1691, London, England
Robert Boyle was the youngest son of the Earl of Cork. He is best known for his experiments with the air pump, which led to a law of physics being named after him. In his youth, he went to Florence where the Medicis were still influential in artistic and esoteric circles. He also studied demonology in Geneva, where he spent twenty-one months of his life. He was one of the first to support the Stuarts when Charles II returned to the English throne. While living in London, one of his visitors was Cosimo III de Medici, who became the ruler of Florence. One of his closest friends was Isaac Newton, to whom he taught the principles of alchemy, which was a life-long interest of his. He wrote two treatises on this subject between 1675 and 1677: *Incalescence of Quicksilver with Gold* and *An Historical Account of a Degradation of Gold*.

Sir Isaac Newton born December 25, 1642 [January 4, 1643, New Style], Woolsthorpe, Lincolnshire, England, died March 20 [March 31], 1727, London
It is interesting that Dan Brown concentrates so much upon Sir Isaac Newton in *The Da Vinci Code*. Best remembered in the twenty-first century as a mathematician and as the greatest influence on theoretical physics until Einstein, Newton was a Priory of Sion dark horse of the highest order. He was educated at Cambridge and elected to the Royal Society in

1672, becoming president in 1703. He formed a close relationship with Nicolas Fatio de Duillier, who was a Genevan aristocrat leading a peripatetic life throughout Europe, and was possibly a spy against Louis XIV of France. Newton became Master of the Royal Mint in 1699, and in 1701 became the Member of Parliament for Cambridge University. He was also a close friend of Jean Desaguliers, who was responsible for the rapid spread of Freemasonry throughout Europe. Although he was perhaps not a Freemason himself, Newton was a member of an association known as "The Gentleman's Club of Spalding" of which Alexander Pope was also a member. Newton started what he considered to be his greatest work, *The Chronology of Ancient Kingdoms Amended* in 1689. He believed that much of the divine wisdom contained within Judaism had filtered down to Pythagoras. In addition to practicing alchemy through his association with Robert Boyle, he also studied sacred geometry and numerology.

Charles Nodier born *April 29, 1780, Besançon, France, died Jan. 27, 1844, Paris*
Nodier had neither noble blood nor contact with any of the families who figure in the Priory of Sion documents. He fell out of favor with the authorities in his youth after writing a satirical poem about Napoleon.[3] Upon moving to Paris in 1824, he became one of the leading lights in Parisian literary society, entertaining such fellow writers as Victor Hugo and Alfred de Musset, who were to become important in the Romantic movement. He was a prolific writer, known best these days for his short stories. His admission to the Académie Française in 1833 consolidated Romanticism as a respected style of literature.

Victor Hugo born *Feb. 26, 1802, Besançon, France, died May 22, 1885, Paris*
Victor Hugo was a poet, novelist, dramatist and the most important of the French Romantic writers. He is best known outside France for his novels *Notre-Dame de Paris* and *Les Misérables*. His father was in Napoleon's army, but had great

---

[3] There is evidence that Abbé Seiyes encouraged Napoleon to marry Josephine Beauhamais because she was of Merovingian descendant.

sympathy with those who conspired against him. Victor Hugo knew Nodier from an early age and Nodier's knowledge of Gothic architecture inspired the setting for The Hunchback of Notre-Dame. Charles Nodier and Victor Hugo founded a literary salon at the Arsenal Library where Nodier worked, known as "the Cenacle." It is possible that the Cenacle was a cover for the Priory of Sion. It included Romantics, artists, surrealists and Symbolists and they adopted "Et in Arcadia Ego" as their properly elegiac and romantic motto. Hugo married in 1822 at l'Église de Saint-Sulpice. He traveled for some years with Nodier and was pall-bearer at Nodier's funeral in 1845. Although deeply religious, Hugo had highly unorthodox views on the Catechism and was deeply attracted to Gnostic, Cabalistic and Hermetic philosophies. He respected Napoleon, but Hugo was a strong monarchist and in favor of the Bourbon line being reinstated. He saw this only as a temporary measure however. He supported in particular the constitutional King, Louis-Philippe, who had risen to power in the July revolution of 1831. Louis-Philippe was married to the niece of Maximilian de Lorraine, a previous Priory of Sion Grand Master and member of the Habsburg-Lorraine line. Much of Victor Hugo's verse was overtly political, but he also wanted to be the "sonorous echo" of the time and wrote of the social problems of his day.

Claude Debussy born Aug. 22, 1862, Saint-Germain-en-Laye, France, died March 25, 1918, Paris
Although he was from a poor background, Debussy rose to prominence quickly. During his youth he came under the patronage of a Russian millionairess, Nadezhda Filaretovna von Meck, who employed him to play duets with her and her children. He traveled extensively with her and met many influential people at that time. He was of a very secretive nature and it has therefore been difficult to establish how strong his connections were with the Priory of Sion families. The main musical influence in his life was Richard Wagner. He said of Wagner that he was "a wonderful sunset that had been mistaken for a dawn." His work was the musical equivalent of Impressionist and Symbolist painting and

writing. His best-known works include *Clair de Lune* and *Prelude to the Afternoon of a Faun*. He set a number of Victor Hugo's works to music. Amongst those he got to know were Émile Hoffet, and through him, Bérenger Saunière, as well as the eminent singer Emma Calvé, who possibly had a romantic relationship with Saunière. Debussy was heavily involved in the occult scene of Paris. At the soirées of the symbolist poet, Stéphane Mallarmé, he also met Oscar Wilde, W.B. Yeats, Paul Valéry, André Gide and Marcel Proust.

Jean Cocteau born July 5, 1889, *Maisons-Laffitte, near Paris, France, died Oct. 11, 1963, Milly-la-Forêt, near Paris*

Jean Cocteau was a French poet, librettist, novelist, actor, film director, and painter. He was known by the nickname of The Frivolous Poet for years after a poem he had written by the same name at the age of fifteen. He was later given the nickname "King of Poets" by his friend Apollinaire. It was Apollinaire who first used the expression "surreal" referring to Cocteau's work on the Ballet Russe. Cocteau had a justified reputation as a libertine, however the fact that he came from an affluent and influential family would have helped him to be selected as Grand Master. He was also good friends with Jean Hugo, the great-grandson of Victor Hugo and Claude Debussy, his predecessor as Grand Master of the Priory. His films Orpheus and Testament of Orpheus have strong Priory of Sion undertones and his murals in the churches of Nôtre Dame de France in London and the Chapel of St. Peter in Villefranche-sur-Mer also appear to contain Priory secrets. In fact, some of his works may have been made at the request of the Priory of Sion. He was a favorite with the French president General de Gaulle and de Gaulle's brother asked Cocteau to make a national address on the general state of France. Charles de Gaulle is suspected to have been a member of the Priory of Sion at some point.

Jean Cocteau was the Grand Master until his death in 1963. When Pierre Plantard de Saint-Claire spoke to Baigent, Leigh and Lincoln in 1979, he was Secretary-General. He apparently took up the office on January 17, 1981, and apparently stepped down in 1984. It is not known who was in office between Cocteau's death and Plantard's Grand Mastership, although Baigent, Leigh and Lincoln were told in 1979 that it had been an influential ecclesiastic named Abbé François Ducaud-Bourget, although he denied it.

The Present Situation

When the Priory of Sion was evicted from Orleans in 1619 it faded from history. The next time there is a record of the Priory of Sion's existence is in 1956 when it was listed in the French *Journal Official*, a weekly government publication in which all societies and organizations declare themselves.[4] However, the Priory of Sion claims to have been involved in various historical events in which it appeared to have an interest throughout the intervening period. It is certain that at least one organization, the Compagnie de Saint-Sacrement of seventeenth century France (discussed later on) operated in the background.

Baigent, Leigh and Lincoln conducted a series of interviews with Pierre Plantard de Saint-Clair when researching their books. Many of these took place at a brasserie called La Tipia on the rue de Rome in Paris. Plantard's answers were enigmatic and sometimes misleading, as is typical of much Priory of Sion information. For instance, he told them that he had been imprisoned by the Gestapo from October 1943 until February 1944 for his involvement in the French Resistance, but no record has been found of this.

They were able to establish that he had run a magazine named *Vaincre* during the Second World War. It dealt not in French Resistance matters, but mythology and various esoteric subjects and appeared to serve as the publication of an organization known as "Alpha Galates." The prime interest of Alpha Galates was chivalry and in structure it seemed to be identical to the Priory of Sion. Indeed, it probably was

---

[4] The Priory of Sion statutes published in 1956 state that the Priory of Sion had a total of 9,841 members divided into nine grades. It consisted of 729 provinces, 27 commanderies, and the top level of hierarchy was an Arch referred to as "Kyria." The Grand Master is known as the "Nautonnier."

the Priory of Sion. *Vaincre* ostensibly supported the Vichy government of the time and included a hymn to Marshal Henri Phillippe Pétain in its first edition. It has to be borne in mind, however, that all publications were subject to the scrutiny of the Nazi censorship machine and Plantard later claimed that the magazine was a secret Resistance journal containing messages and codes that only Resistance members could understand. As M. Plantard was a later associate of General Charles de Gaulle, who did not tolerate Nazi collaborators, it is unlikely that his apparent support of the Vichy government was genuine.

One of the main objectives of Alpha Galates/the Priory of Sion was the formation of a United States of Europe which would be a bulwark between the United States of America and the Soviet Union, as well as a separate entity of great power. Perhaps they have succeeded: Europe now has its own currency and to a large degree, its own federal government. The emblem for a United Europe that was suggested by the Priory of Sion as early as the 1940s was a circle of stars, which is what is now on the European Union flag.

In the United States the newly-formed CIA had the same idea. Millions of dollars were poured into Europe by the American government during the 1950s and 1960s to prevent the "spread of the reds" and to popularize the idea of a united Europe. The CIA and the Vatican have always had a strong relationship. CIA money was freely dispersed to bishops and monseigneurs, including Giovanni Montini, the future Pope Paul VI, to fund various cultural activities and enterprises towards these ends.

The Algerian Debacle
In 1957 France was in turmoil because of the war for independence in Algeria. To protect French interests in Algeria, the Comités de Salut Public (Committees of Public Safety) were formed. The person considered suitable to head these committees was Charles de Gaulle and from that time on they worked to make de Gaulle president of France by any means possible. They received support from many influential sources, including Marshall Alphonse Juin, reputedly a mem-

ber of the Priory of Sion. De Gaulle allowed the Algerian Committees to believe that he supported their cause.

In 1958, the newly elected French government said that the only way to get out of the crisis in Algeria was to grant Algeria independence. The Committees appealed to de Gaulle to take over the government but he remained detached from the situation.

The Committees for Public Safety then began to assert their position in France. The word on the street was that a military coup in France was imminent. The government then resigned and de Gaulle stepped into power. At this point there appears to have been a conflict of interest between the Committees in Algeria, who wanted Algeria to stay French and the Committees in France, who saw the installation of de Gaulle as much more important.

De Gaulle was in awkward position. He had achieved the Presidency by supporting the continued colonial status of Algeria and yet he was about to negotiate independence with the Algerian leaders. Because of this decision, for the rest of life he lived in fear of assassination at the hands of former Algerian committee members who considered de Gaulle's actions to be treacherous.

The main danger was, however, from the French Committees of Public Safety whose opposition could have caused much more trouble. The public relations operation to prevent this from happening was conducted by Pierre Plantard de Saint-Clair, who formed the Central Paris Committee with the intention of taking over the other Committees.

CIRCUIT
Later on, two series of a new magazine were published by the Priory of Sion. It was called CIRCUIT, which was the acronym for "Chevalerie d'Institutions et Règles Catholiques, d'Union Indépendante et Traditionaliste" ("Chivalry of Catholic Rules and Institutions of the Independent and Traditionalist Union"). It was the subtitle

which the Priory of Sion identified itself as to the French police when it registered in 1956. The first series consisted of an array of esoteric material similar to that in *Vaincre*, as well as what appears to be information regarding a low-cost housing association. The later 1959 series of CIRCUIT, however, lists its director as Pierre Plantard. It says that it is the magazine for an organization called the "Federation of French Forces." But no information on such organization has ever been found. Interestingly, however, the contact details given were those which Anne Lea Hisler – the first wife of M. Plantard – said were those of the Secretariat-General of the Committees of Public Safety in metropolitan France. It therefore appears that the Federation of French Forces was the administrative arm of a continuation of the Committees.

In addition to sharing many of the themes of *Vaincre*, there are also articles in CIRCUIT about vines, viticulture, and the wine trade which could clearly be a coded reference to a genealogy, as wine, in the Christian tradition, represents blood, and vines, a bloodline. As Jesus identified himself as the Vine, it is reasonable to suppose that this specific use of the symbol represents his progeny.

The "Truth" behind Pierre Plantard de Saint-Clair

Whether the Priory of Sion exists today after the resignation of Pierre Plantard de Saint-Clair as its Grand Master is a matter of speculation. He told Baigent, Leigh and Lincoln that he resigned in 1984 because of the intractable situation caused by an infiltrating "Anglo-American" contingent, which wanted to move the Priory's goals in another direction. Another reason for his resignation had to do with inflammatory information that was about to be published in a book called *The Scandals of the Prieuré de Sion*, written by "Cornelius." Baigent, Leigh and Lincoln received a tract regarding this book, which purportedly detailed various shady financial transactions involving the Priory of Sion, a prominent Italian politician and bankers in the USA. Cardinal Jean Danielou, an erstwhile friend of Jean Cocteau who had probably met Pierre Plantard, was found dead in mysterious circumstances in 1974. "Cornelius" wrote that Danielou was involved financially with the Priory of Sion. He also suggested links between the Priory of Sion, the Italian Mafia, and a secret society known as "P2" (see Chapter Ten for more on P2). He also says that two days after Plantard was elected Grand Master, a high-ranking member of the Priory had a meeting with Licio Gelli, the Grand Master of P2, at the previously mentioned "La Tipia." However, although the tract written by "Cornelius" was widely distributed, none of the allegations were substantiated and could possibly be challenged successfully in a libel court.

Although Pierre Plantard maintained that he was descended from the Merovingian King Dagobert II, some think that Plantard's royal lineage was based upon a forgery. According to the BBC television program *Timewatch*, his name was simply inserted into a genealogy that had been copied verbatim from a history magazine. Some say that he was descended from a sixteenth century walnut farmer and that he only added the particle "de Saint-Clair" to his name in 1964. There is also speculation that the revived Priory of Sion was purely of his own invention. Certainly since his resignation, nobody has laid claim to the organization. Dan Brown says that the Priory of Sion is still based in France, but some suspect that it has re-emerged in Barcelona.

It is difficult to see the truth through the all-pervading smoke-screen that has shrouded the Priory of Sion for centuries. But given its history to date, there is no reason to believe that it has packed its bags and gone away. It is more likely that it is playing a caretaker role behind the scenes and could rise again in any form at any time.

Chapter Three
The Davidic and Merovingian Bloodlines

AFTER DETAILED AND LENGTHY RESEARCH, THE AUTHORS OF *HOLY BLOOD, HOLY GRAIL* (MICHAEL BAIGENT, RICHARD LEIGH AND HENRY LINCOLN) REACHED SOME FASCINATING CONCLUSIONS ABOUT THE CHRISTIAN FAITH AND WESTERN HISTORY IN PARTIC-ULAR. THEY DO NOT MAINTAIN THAT THESE CONCLU-SIONS ARE 100% ACCURATE, BUT THE EVIDENCE THAT THEY MARSHAL IS COMPELLING.

The concept of the Holy Grail being the bloodline of Jesus Christ is one of the basic themes of *The Da Vinci Code*. Belief in it negates the purpose of the present-day Christian hierarchy and it would be a matter of no surprise that efforts would be made to suppress proof of its existence at any cost. If accepted, it destroys the fabric of the Church itself, challenging not only its doctrines, but its legitimacy as the minister of Christ's church. Monarchies and governments, past and present, legit-imized throughout history by representatives of the Christian denominations, would be rendered invalid.

Some of the Priory of Sion documents state that the Merovingian pedigree can be traced back to the Old Testament and ancient Troy. They are suspected of being from one Israelite tribe in particular – that which was head-ed by Benjamin. Their territory embraced what is now the area around Jerusalem before the city became the capital of David and Solomon.

However, the Benjamin tribe fell out with the other tribes of Israel who were then forbidden from giving their daughters to a Benjamite man in marriage, because of the Benjamites' support for the worshippers of the heathen god Belial. This god is often associated with the bull or calf, similar to the Golden Calf that the Benjamites are said in the Bible to have worshipped. The tribe recovered from this problem eventually and went on to supply Israel with its first King, Saul.

Despite their restored position, by this time it appears that many of the Benjamites had gone into exile, and some evidence shows that the place they chose to land was the central area of Greece: Arcadia. From there they progressed into present-day Germany and intermarried with the Teuton tribes. Eventually these became the Sicambrian Franks, from whom the Merovingians descended. As discussed in Chapter Two, before Godfroi de Bouillon left on the First Crusade, he was so confident that he would be asked to become King of Jerusalem that he rid himself of all his property. This confidence would have arisen through his knowledge that his Merovingian ancestry would place him in a better position than anyone else for the title.

The Benjamites would no doubt have asked their sea-faring allies, the Phoenicians, for help in achieving their exile. In *The Greek Myths*, Robert Graves writes about the myth *Belus and the Danaids*: "This myth records the early arrival in Greece of the Helladic colonists from Palestine by way of Rhodes, and their introduction of agriculture into the Peloponnese." The cult of the Mother Goddess Ishtar (known in Phoenicia as Astarte), which originated in Sumeria, became the established cult of the Arcadian, and thrived for centuries.

Other evidence points to the similarities of the Spartans to the Merovingians. They both believed that their long hair gave them their strength upon reaching manhood, a trait also attributed to the Biblical character Samson. Also, it states in *Maccabees 1* that: "It has been found in writing concerning the Spartans and the Jews that they are brethren and are of the family of Abraham."

Trade routes throughout southern France and up the Rhône had been established by the Phoenicians. Semitic objects found in this area indicate the dynastic alliances that had arisen through the intermarrying of the Phoenician kings and those of Israel and Judah in the ninth century BC.

A Jewish colony was established in Rome between 106 and 48 BC and after the sack of Jerusalem in 70 AD, a large number of Jews escaped to both Italy and France. Additionally, there were many Jewish slaves who had accompanied their masters throughout Europe and who were eventually freed to form their own communities.

The first time that the Magdalene appears in the New Testament with any real significance is when she is described as being the first person to see Christ after the Resurrection – one reason why she is revered as a saint in France and other places where churches are dedicated to her. One of the most persistent stories about the Holy Grail is that it was brought by the Magdalene to France where, according to fourth century legend, she landed at Marseilles. This is the French port city on the Mediterranean where the river Rhône, an established Phoenician trade route, reaches the sea.

The original Grail romance was written by Chrétien de Troyes. He was associated with the court of the count of Champagne and his story was called *Le Roman de Perceval* or *Le Conte del Graal*. The tale was written in about 1188, which was also the year, of course, that the Priory of Sion divided from the Order of the Temple, and the year that Jerusalem fell.

In *Le Conte del Graal*, the main character, Perceval, described as the "Son of the Widow Lady," leaves his mother in search of fame and fortune. He meets a mysterious fisherman, the "Fisher King," who invites him to stay in his castle for the night. During the course of the evening, the golden Grail appears, studded with gems, carried by a damsel. Perceval does not realize that he is supposed to ask the Grail a question and the question that he is supposed to ask is "Whom does the Grail serve?" In fairness, he can be excused for there was no way of knowing that this is what was expected of him. However, when he wakes up in the morning, as a result of his omission, which had clearly been taken very seriously, he discovers that the castle is deserted and the surrounding land has been destroyed. He also discovers that the "Fisher King" is his own uncle. At this point, it is hard to believe that anyone could blame him for feeling disillusioned with just about everything and Perceval says that he can no longer continue loving or believing in God.

Chrétien died before the poem was completed. Some say that he died mysteriously in a fire that broke out in Troyes that year, 1188. During the next few years the idea of the Grail spread quickly throughout Europe and became most closely associated with the legend of King Arthur. Until this time, however, it had not been associated with Jesus.

The Merovingians
The Merovingians ruled much of present-day France and Germany between the fifth and seventh centuries. The beginning of this time coincides with not only the Grail stories, but with the era of King Arthur, who was so central to many of these tales. There was never any question that the Merovingians were the rightful rulers of the Franks. They were not "created" as kings. The sons who were entitled became kings automatically on their twelfth birthdays. Their role was not to govern – that was left to the "Mayors of the Palace." They were simply expected to exist as representatives of the role, holding similar power and status to a twenty-first century constitutional monarch. They were also allowed the delights of polygamy and sometimes took great advantage of this privilege.

The origin of the Merovingian family name comes from that of their progenitor, Mérovée (also styled "Merovech" or "Meroveus"). The name is reminiscent of both the French word for "mother" and the French and Latin words for "sea." The legend is that Mérovée was born of two fathers – the story that is told is no doubt allegorical and refers to the alliance of two dynasties through his birth. It was said that his mother was already pregnant by her husband when she went swimming in the sea. She was seduced by a sea creature who impregnated her for a second time. When Mérovée was born therefore, the blood of two sources, that of his Frankish father, the ruler, and that of a "sea animal" ran through his veins.

From that time on, the Merovingians had a reputation for the occult and the supernatural. They were looked upon as priest-kings, much as the Egyptian pharaohs were regarded. The healing powers they were said to have possessed extended even to the tassels of their robes, which were believed to be of particular curative powers. As we shall see in Chapter Four, after the death of Bérenger Saunière a procession of people passed by his robed corpse, each removing a tassel from it. The Merovingian kings were said to have had a certain birthmark that took the form of a Templar type red cross, either over the heart or between the shoulder blades.

King Childeric I was the son of Mérovée and the father of Merovingian King Clovis. When his tomb was found in the seventeenth century in the Ardennes region of Belgium, it contained such items of sorcery as a severed horse's head, a golden bull's head and a crystal ball.

One of the abiding symbols of the Merovingians was the bee. Hundreds of pure gold bees were found in King Childeric's tomb. The custom endured through the centuries. When Napoleon was crowned emperor in 1804, he made sure that golden bees were attached to his coronation robes. He was fascinated by the Merovingians and commissioned their genealogies to be compiled in order to find out whether the dynasty had survived after it had been deposed. These formed the basis of the genealogies found in the Priory of Sion documents.

The Merovingians claimed two different origins: from Noah, and from Troy. The latter would explain place names in France such as Troyes and Paris. Also, according to Homer, there were a number of Arcadians at Troy. The bear was considered to be sacred in Arcadia and the forbears of the Merovingians, Sicambrian Franks, also held the bear in great esteem. Another possible connection is that the Welsh word for "bear" is "arth" which may explain the origin of King Arthur's name.

By the time the Sicambrians had moved into present day France to escape the invasion of the Huns, they had already established themselves as a sophisticated society which had developed along Roman lines. Therefore the Merovingians, who inherited their culture, could be perceived to follow the Roman imperial modal. The culture of the Franks thrived and prospered under the Merovingian dynasty from this point onwards. The Merovingians accumulated enormous wealth during this period, and the equal-armed cross that their coins bore was exactly the same as that used during the Crusades for the Frankish Kingdom of Jerusalem.

Clovis I is perhaps the most famous of the Merovingian monarchs, as it was he who introduced Roman Christianity into France. His Catholic wife had given him more than a little encouragement to go in this direction, but it is likely that there was another reason for his being won over to the idea.

Christianity at this time took many different forms. The Roman Church was in constant conflict with the Celtic Church. In 496 AD, Clovis had a number of secret meetings with Saint Rémy. This led to a deal being struck between Clovis and the Roman Church in which Clovis would act as the strong arm of the Church. In return for this, he was to rule over what had been Constantine's Holy Roman Empire, which the Visigoths and Vandals had destroyed.

It was of enormous importance to the Roman Church that this should work as it would mean a new Roman and Christian Empire, administered by the secular Merovingian dynasty. And so Clovis was baptized by Saint Rémy at Rheims in France. In this way, the Roman Church was making a pact not only with Clovis, but with all of his descendants.

Clovis carried out his side of the bargain enthusiastically. He increased the size of his empire to embrace much of what is now France and Germany. He was particularly keen to defeat the Visigoths and eventually did so at the Battle of Vouillé. The Visigoths were turned further and further back and they finally established themselves in the Razès area, at Rhédae – the present village of Rennes-le-Château.

After Clovis' death, his realm was divided, according to the tradition at the time, amongst his four sons. This led to a breakdown of the cohesion that had previously existed, and gave the Mayors of the Palace the perfect opportunity to gain more power. However, they had Dagobert II to contend with.

Dagobert was born in 651 and when Clovis, his father, died in 656, all efforts were made to prevent him from inheriting Austrasia, the north-eastern realm of Clovis. The leading Mayor of the Palace of the time, Grimoald, kidnapped Dagobert as soon as his father died and managed to persuade the court first that Dagobert was dead, and second that Clovis had wanted Grimoald's son to inherit the throne. So convincing was he that even Dagobert's mother believed him.

However, Grimoald had been unable to bring himself to murder Dagobert and had taken him to the Bishop of Poitiers, who had the child King exiled to Ireland. Here he grew up and was educated at the monastery of Slane near Dublin. He married a Celtic princess, Mathilde, and moved to York in northern England, where he got to know Saint Wilfred, the Bishop of York. At this time, the Merovingian alliance with the Roman Church was not as strong as it had been at the time of Clovis.

Wilfred was very keen to bring the Celtic and Roman churches together, which both sides had agreed upon at the Council of Whitby in 664. However, it seems that Wilfred also recognized the valuable potential of Dagobert – the rightful King of Austrasia – returning to France and reclaiming the land as the militant representative of the Church.

Dagobert's wife died in 670 and Wilfred was swift to ensure that Dagobert's next wife was chosen with care. She was

Giselle de Razès, the daughter of the Count of Razès and the niece of the King of the Visigoths. This alliance between the Merovingians and the Visigoths would not only have brought much of France under the same rule, it would have empowered Rome over the Visigoths.

They married at the church of St. Magdeleine in Rennes-le-Château. Having had four daughters through his two marriages, Dagobert now became the father to a son in 676 – Sigisbert IV.

After living three years at Rennes-le-Château, Dagobert was proclaimed the King of Austrasia. He quickly set about re-establishing order throughout his new kingdom and in so doing greatly increased his wealth.

He did not, however, live up to Wilfred's expectations, angering the Roman Church by attempting to limit its influence in his realm. Through his marriage into the Visigoth dynasty, he also acquired much of what is now the Languedoc region in southern France. The Visigoths had never felt allegiance to Rome. They preferred the heretical "Arian" form of Christianity which insisted that Christ was an ordinary human being who had been born as all other men and Dagobert seemed to be following their example.

Therefore, inevitably, with his new-found wealth and lands, he developed enemies. He also caused the resentment of the rulers of neighboring Frankish lands, some of whom had connections in Dagobert's court that could be dangerous to him. One of these was his Mayor to the Palace, the treacherous Pepin the Fat.

The larger of Dagobert's two palaces was at Stenay in the Ardennes. Nearby was the Forest of Woëvres, where, as we learned in Chapter Two, Dagobert went hunting on December 23, 679. It was while he was sleeping under a tree that his godson supposedly crept up to him, and under Pepin's orders, lanced him in the eye, killing him. The murdering band then returned to Stenay where, it was believed, they slaughtered the rest of Dagobert's family. The Roman Church wasted no time in commending the action. However, perhaps through guilt, they canonized Dagobert in 872, when his remains were moved to the graveyard of a church which was renamed "the Church of Saint Dagobert." They even gave him his own feast day, on December 23rd. This day also happened to be sacred to the Benjamite tribe. The Roman Catholic Church has always been unable or unwilling to explain why he was canonized.

From the day of his burial in the Church of Saint Dagobert, his grave has been a destination of pilgrimage for various significant historical figures including the Duke of Lorraine, the grandfather of Godfroi de Bouillon. The church was destroyed during the French Revolution and most of the relics of Saint Dagobert disappeared. Today only what is believed to be his skull remains, and it is held at a convent at Mons. Curiously some years later, a poem entitled "de Sancta Dagoberto martyre prose" appeared. Its message was that Dagobert had been martyred for some reason and it was found at the Abbey of Orval.

Dagobert's assassination effectively marked the end of the Merovingian era. After the death of Dagobert, the Merovingian dynasty fell into decline, although they managed to hang onto much of their status for nearly a hundred more years. However, many of the monarchs were too young to be effective, and were unable to defend themselves against the relentless ambitions of the Mayors of the Palace. Childeric III died childless in 754 and that was the clearest sign that the dynasty's flame had expired.

Pepin the Fat, who ordered the assassination of Dagobert, had his son Charles Martel placed in a position of leadership. Despite his excellent military reputation, and the fact that the opportunity was there for him, he seems to have avoided claiming the throne, perhaps through respect for the rights of the Merovingians. After Charles Martel died in 741, his son, Pepin III who was Mayor of the Palace to King Childeric III, went to the Pope with a delegation and asked the question, "Who should be King? The man who actually holds the power, or he, though called King, has no power at all." The Pope agreed that Pepin should be made King and thus broke the agreement that had been established with Clovis. Childeric was sent to a monastery, where he died four years later and Pepin was established firmly on the throne of the Franks.

Pepin III's coronation in 754 was conducted according to new rules which ensured kings would be created instead of simply acknowledged. This was done in accordance with the fraudulent document called the *Donation of Constantine*, which is discussed fully in Chapter Five on Constantine the Great. The Carolingian dynasty started at this point, named after Charles Martel, although it is more closely associated with his descendant Charlemagne, who in 800 was proclaimed Holy Roman Emperor – a title that had previously belonged solely to the Merovingian kings.

Just before Pepin III was crowned, he married a Merovingian princess, presumably to legitimize himself in his own eyes, propelling the Merovingian genes once again in their rightful direction. Charlemagne married similarly. In fact his misgivings even seemed to affect his coronation. He seemed determined to give the impression that he was bashful about becoming Holy Roman Emperor. The ceremony had been fixed so that it appeared that the Pope was crowning him without Charlemagne's prior knowledge. Charlemagne accepted the crown expressing the mock shock that film stars show when being awarded an Oscar. To add credence to the performance he insisted that he would never have entered the Roman cathedral if he had known that was going to happen.

The betrayal of Clovis by the assassination of Dagobert II has been the greatest source of anguish for the Priory of Sion and the Merovingian descendants. However, there seems to have been an attempt to mitigate the insult. Thus the Carolingian royal family (the family of Emperor Charlemagne) married Merovingian princesses in order to legitimize themselves. Dagobert's son, Sigisbert, was the ancestor of Guillem de Gellone, ruler of the Jewish kingdom of Septimania in southern France and later of Godfroi de Bouillon, who captured Jerusalem during the Crusades. Thereby the bloodline of Jesus Christ, the Davidic line, was restored back to the throne that had been rightfully its own since the time of the Old Testament.

The Conclusion

There can be little reasonable doubt that Jesus was actually married. As we see will in Chapter Eight on the marriage of Jesus Christ, the heir to the Davidic line was required by law to marry. Not only that – they were required to sire at least two sons (an "heir and a spare," as they say about the British royal family.) Such present-day lifestyle choices as live-in partners or single-sex relationships simply did not exist in first century Judea. Marriage for those of the Davidic line was ritualized to the extent of making redundant any necessity for romanticism. The necessity of continuing the survival of the line in such a rural and, at the same time, *persecuted* community was paramount to all. Jesus and his wife, Mary Magdalene, after fleeing from the Holy Land, had several children who were brought up in a Jewish community in southern France. Jesus had been known as a "fisher" from the time that he was admitted into the priesthood in the Order of Melchizedek, as described in *Hebrews* 5. In this way the House of Judah became a dynasty of Priest-Kings who were referred to in the Grail mythology as the "Fisher Kings." The line of descent from these Fisher Kings became the French House del Acqs. The name "Acqs" comes from *aquae* meaning "waters" and the family was a major influence in the French area of Aquitaine. The Merovingian dynasty came from this line and were the Counts of Toulouse and Narbonne and the Princes of Septimania Midi in what is now south-west France. In the fifth century, it seems that the descendants of these children married into the royal line of the Franks, bringing about the Merovingian dynasty.

As we have seen before in this chapter, the Roman Catholic Church made a pact with Clovis, one of the Merovingian kings, in 496 AD, in which it pledged itself for all time to

the Merovingian bloodline. This was presumably because
they recognized the true identity of the Merovingian bloodline. Clovis was offered the title of Holy Roman Emperor (or
"New Constantine," as the title was then phrased), and therefore did not become King, although of course, by Merovingian
succession traditions, he was recognized as such.

It seems conclusive that the Church played a part in the
assassination of Dagobert II and was never able to forgive
itself for this. This resulted in the betrayal of the
Merovingians and it was vital to the Church that this knowledge was not widely known, as it would have played
straight into the hands of Rome's enemies. Rome was, however, unable to suppress the truth completely and one of the
ways in which the truth of the matter was revealed was allegorically, through such literature as the romances of the
Holy Grail.

Thus the Holy Grail had two simultaneous identities. The
first was that of the "Sang Real": the "Real" or "Royal"
blood of which the Knights Templar were guardians.
Second, it would have been the vessel or receptacle of Jesus'
blood (or rather semen) – that is, the womb of Mary
Magdalene. Thus many of the churches that are supposedly
dedicated to the "Virgin" Mary in the form of "Black
Virgins" or "Black Madonnas" were in fact been dedicated
to the Magdalene.

The Holy Grail may also have been, literally speaking, the
treasure that had been taken in 70 AD when the emperor Titus
plundered the Temple of Jerusalem. This vast wealth eventually found its way to the Pyrenees mountain range, and is today
reputed to be in the hands of the Priory of Sion. As well as this
treasure, the Temple of Solomon is likely to have contained
birth certificates, marriage certificates and other documents
relating to the royal line of Israel. It would no doubt also give
evidence of Jesus Christ's claim to be King of the Jews.

There is no evidence that Titus or his soldiers found such
documentation. Logic, however, would lead us to believe

that the soldiers would have been happy to carry away the copious amounts of gold and jewels that were available, thus leaving the way clear for the more sensitive documentation to be hidden away.

The descendants of Jesus Christ had reached positions of influence and importance by 1100 in Europe and also, through Godfroi de Bouillon, in Palestine. Even though they may have been well aware of their ancestry, they may not have been able to prove it without the documentary or other proof that remained at the Temple of Solomon.[5] This would explain the excavations that the Knights Templar made around the area of the Temple at that time. On the basis of the evidence that Leigh, Baigent, and Lincoln found, it appears that not only were the Knights Templar sent to Jerusalem to find something, but that they did, in fact, succeed, and returned with it to England. It is unclear what happened to it then, but it is known that the fourth Grand Master of the Order of the Temple, Bertrand de Blanchefort, concealed something near Rennes-le-Château and German miners were brought to construct a hiding place. There is speculation over what this "something" may have been, ranging from Jesus' marriage certificate and/or birth certificates of his children to his mummified body. Any of these may have been passed to the heretical Cathar sect in the area of Languedoc near Rennes-le-Château, who were massacred mercilessly by 30,000 of the Pope's soldiers in 1209. Treasure was hidden at the Cathar stronghold of Montségur, which was under siege for ten months until March 1244.

Once the Merovingians re-established themselves in Jerusalem, they could better afford to make the facts known. This explains why the Grail romances, which were associated so closely with the Knights Templar, started appearing at this time. Eventually no doubt the full truth of the Merovingian kings would have come out and they would

[5] There was a royal tradition that the bloodline of both Godfroi and Boudouin de Bouillon was "founded upon the Rock of Sion" and equal in status to the foremost of European dynasties. Both the New Testament and later Freemasonry maintain that the "Rock of Sion" was in fact Jesus.

have ruled extensively over Europe, replacing the Pope and making Jerusalem the capital of the Christian world. If Jesus had been accepted as a mortal prophet, a priest-King and the descendant of the Davidic line by Christians, he may also have been accepted by the Muslims and Jews. That would obviously have changed Middle East history drastically.

However, this was not the course of history and the Frankish kingdom of Jerusalem did not succeed. With the loss of the Holy Land in 1291 to the Muslims, the Merovingians were sidelined and the Knights Templar rendered redundant. Since that time, the Roman Catholic Church has continued to strengthen at the expense of the truth.

The Australian "Royal Family"

On January 3, 2004, Britain's Channel 4 TV showed a documentary, *Britain's Real Monarch*, in which Tony Robinson, perhaps best known for playing "Baldrick" in the BBC TV series *Blackadder*, presented evidence that had been discovered by the historian Michael K. Jones regarding the ancestors of the present British royal family.

On the death of Edward IV, his young son, also called Edward, reigned briefly but was never crowned. He and his brother Richard, Duke of York, were taken to the Tower of London, where their uncle Richard, who was to become Richard III, acted as their Lord Protector. It was then pronounced, on dubious grounds, that the young princes were illegitimate. Shortly afterwards, they disappeared and were never seen again. The accusing finger of history has pointed at Richard III ever since, although there is no conclusive proof of his involvement. However, he is alleged to have had his two young nephews smothered to death and in 1674 two skeletons of boys were found in the Tower and believed to be those of the young princes. The depiction of Richard III as a hunchbacked and evil man is largely the responsibility of Shakespeare and is thought to have originated as Tudor propaganda. For centuries the English King Richard III has been the subject of controversy. Some claim that as he was the last Plantagenet

King, he was the last "Grail King" of England. This could explain the propaganda in Tudor times, as both Henry VIII and his daughter Elizabeth I were painfully aware of their comparatively humble ancestry.

The true story, according to Tony Robinson, is quite different. He maintains that Edward IV himself was illegitimate and therefore the crown should have gone to his brother George, Duke of Clarence. The implications for both British and American history are enormous.

The mother of Edward IV was Cecily Neville. She was called "Proud Cis" because of her legendary feisty temper. Dominic Mancici, who was visiting London in 1483, reported that Cecily "fell into a frenzy," making the incredible, self-deprecating accusation that Edward IV was illegitimate and that she would be prepared to swear to that effect before a public enquiry. It was an extraordinary thing for a mother to admit to. There had been a rumor that she had had an affair with an English archer named Blaybourne, who may have been the real father. Edward IV was tall and bore no physical resemblance to either his siblings or his ancestors. He looked, in fact, like a well-built archer. Blaybourne was based in the garrison at Rouen in Normandy, France, which is where Cecily and her husband, Richard, the Duke of York, lived. According to conclusive evidence in the archbishopric records at the cathedral of Rouen, Cecily's husband, Richard, was away fighting at Pontoise in another part of France during the five weeks period in which the future Edward IV would have been conceived.

The future Edward IV therefore appears to have been the result of the relationship that Cecily had with Blaybourne. However the matter was never taken very seriously and historians have said that the incident arose because of two reasons. First, Cecily wanted to blacken Edward's name because she hated his wife, Elizabeth Woodville. Second it is said that she was bullied into the admission by her other son, also called Richard, to enhance his chances of becoming King Richard III.

Edward was born in Rouen on April 28, 1442, and although he was the eldest son, he was not legitimate, and therefore not entitled to inherit the throne. Edward IV had his younger brother George, Duke of Clarence, tried for treason and he is thought to have met his end by drowning in a vat of malmsey wine in order to avoid the shame of execution. This means that Richard was the only true heir and successor to the throne immediately following his brother George's death and it helped clear the way for Richard to come to the throne. His cause was therefore a source of inspiration to his soldiers on the field of battle.

The descendants of George, Duke of Clarence were treated despicably. His daughter, Margaret Pole, who should have been Margaret I of England, was beheaded at the age of 68 during the reign of Henry VIII in 1541, based on trumped-up treason charges. Other members of her family were left to waste away in the Tower of London. Her last words were: "Blessed are they who suffer persecution for justice's sake, for theirs is the kingdom of heaven." At the time, the regular executioner was unavailable. His unskilled deputy was unable to perform the execution properly and cleanly, and so just chopped away at her neck until she was dead.

Despite this unseemly death, her bloodline has continued in a direct line from this point on. Non-regal names such as Edith, Barbara and Ian abound in their family tree and the present "King" of England is, in fact, Michael Hastings, a portly Australian man who voted against the continued British constitutional monarchy in Australia, and for a republic. He was neither fazed nor excited upon Tony Robinson telling him of his illustrious title. He left England in 1960 for Australia at the age of seventeen and joined a stocking station agency that traded in livestock and property. He has lived in Jerilderie, New South Wales, which has a population of 1100, since 1966. These days he works at the Australian Rice Research Institute. He and his wife Noelene have five children and five grandchildren – all, like their father, staunch republicans. Michael's eldest son, Simon, is his heir.

We have to consider and accept the fact that monarchy can exist only as a bloodline in modern times. Otherwise it has no significance whatsoever and certainly no connection with what we understand to be democracy. As if the damaging legacy of the *Donation of Constantine* were not enough to contemplate, the illegitimacy of Edward IV means that none of the monarchs of Britain have reigned legitimately!

For example, George III, who was the monarch of Britain at the time of the American War of Independence, was in no position to lose the war in his name. However, since previous monarchs had been unable to hold the colony in their name for the same reasons, perhaps the argument is merely academic.

In turn this means that none of the laws that British monarchs have rubber-stamped or endorsed have any legal meaning. The monarchy has a rough ride in the British press at times but nobody has seriously suggested before that their presence is not valid from the point of view of their bloodline! They should perhaps be grateful that the "legal" occupiers of the British throne are, ironically, so anti-monarchist that their position is likely to remain unthreatened.

It would be interesting, perhaps, to see what Dan Brown would make of this story.

Chapter Four
The Real Saunière and Rennes-le-Château

LATE NINETEENTH CENTURY SOUTHERN FRANCE WAS NOT A PLACE TO MAKE A LOT OF MONEY. NOR WAS IT A PLACE OF GREAT EXCITEMENT. YET IT WAS TO BECOME THE CENTER OF SUCH MYSTERIOUS ACTIVITY AND BAFFLING SUDDEN WEALTH THAT HISTORIANS ARE STILL PUZZLING OVER IT. THE CHIEF PROTAGONIST OF THE EVENTS THAT UNFOLDED THERE WAS BÉRENGER SAUNIÈRE AND THIS IS A NAME THAT WILL RESONATE LOUD AND CLEAR WITH READERS OF *THE DA VINCI CODE*.

Dan Brown names the curate of the Louvre who is found murdered at the beginning of the novel, "Jacques Saunière." No mention is made in the book of any family connection between Jacques and Bérenger Saunière. It is unlikely that Bérenger had a son – at least one that bore his name – as he was the Catholic parish priest of Rennes-le-Château and therefore forbidden to marry.

Rennes-le-Château is a village situated on a mountain peak 25 miles from Carcassonne in southern France. After Dagobert II was assassinated on December 23rd, 679, his son, Sigisbert IV, took refuge at Rennes-le-Château where his mother, Giselle de Razès, came from. A few miles away is the imposing mountain Bézu, on which stand the ruins of a former center of the Knights Templar. About a mile east from Rennes-le-Château lie the ruins of the castle of the Blanchefort family and the home of Bertrand de Blanchefort, the fourth grandmaster of the Knights Templar. The Knights Templar are the so-called "Warrior Monks" who were proclaimed by Pope Innocent II in a Papal Bull in

1139 to owe allegiance only to the Pope and therefore under no obligation to kings and princes. Effectively they constituted an autonomous international empire.

The Discovery

Bérenger Saunière, the priest of Rennes-le-Château, decided to partly renovate the crumbling village church in 1891. It had been consecrated to Mary Magdalene in 1059 and was built on the site of a Visigoth church that dated back to the sixth century.

When the altar stone was removed, Saunière found that one of its supporting pillars was hollow. Inside this column were four parchments kept in two sealed wooden tubes. Two of them appeared to be genealogies. One dated from 1244 and the other from 1644.

The latter two had been written in Latin by one of Saunière's predecessors, Abbé Antoin Bigou, who had been personal priest to the Blanchefort family – important landowners in the area. These parchments dated from the 1780s, and seemed to be written excerpts from the New Testament in Latin. However, in one of the parchments the words were written without spaces, with extra – and at first sight unnecessary – letters added.

In the second parchment some letters were raised above the others. The following decipherment has appeared in French documents written about Rennes-le-Château; the book *Holy Blood, Holy Grail* by Michael Baigent, Richard Leigh and Henry Lincoln; and the BBC films that Henry Lincoln made about the subject:

BERGERE PAS DE TENTATION QUE POUSSIN TENIERS GARDENT LA CLEF PAX DCLXXXI PAR LA CROIX ET CE CHEVAL DE DIEU J'ACHEVE CE DAEMON DE GARDIEN A MIDI POMMES BLEUES.

which translates as:

SHEPHERDESS, NO TEMPTATION THAT POUSSIN, TENIERS, HOLD THE KEY; PEACE 681, BY THE CROSS AND THIS HORSE OF GOD I COMPLETE (OR DESTROY) THIS DAEMON OF THE GUARDIAN AT NOON, BLUE APPLES.

Rather more obvious in the second parchment is the following, spelled out in raised letters:

A DAGOBERT II ROI ET A SION EST CE TRESOR ET IL EST LA MORT.

which translates as:

TO DAGOBERT II, KING, AND TO SION BELONGS THIS TREASURE AND HE IS THERE DEAD.

Saunière was at a loss to understand the parchments, but thought that he could have happened upon something important and therefore took them to the Bishop of Carcassonne. Life was not to be the same for him from that point on. Some speculation suggests that he had been directed to the documents by the Priory of Sion, who enlisted him to act on their behalf.

He was immediately ordered to go to Paris, at the Bishop's expense, where he was told to meet various important authorities of the Catholic Church. He spent three weeks there showing the parchments to Abbé Bieil, the Director General of Saint-Sulpice and his nephew, Émile Hoffet. Hoffet was in his twenties, training for the priesthood and a well-respected scholar of linguistics, cryptography and paleography. He was also involved in occult groups which included the writers Stéphane Mallarmé and Maurice Maeterlink, as well as the composer Claude Debussy. The famous opera singer, Emma Calvé, also mixed in these circles and is reputed to have had an affair with Saunière, or at least a very close friendship with him. In Rennes-le-Château there was once an inscription that read "E. Calve" on a rock near the "Lover's Fountain," along with a heart with an arrow running through it.

While in Paris, Saunière bought reproductions of three paintings from the Louvre. One was *Les Bergers d' Arcadie – The Shepherds of Arcadia* by Nicolas Poussin, one of the painters mentioned in the coded parchments. The other two reproductions were a painting by David Teniers, the other painter mentioned in the parchments, and a portrait of Pope St. Célestin V (Petro de Morrone) who had reigned in 1294.

When Saunière returned to Rennes-le-Château, he continued renovations on the church, discovering a burial chamber in the church that, it is said, contained skeletons. He also turned his attention to the sepulchre of Marie, Marquise d'Hautpol de Blanchefort. This had been designed by Abbé Antoin Bigou and the rearranged letters on the inscription formed an anagram of the code above referring to Poussin and Teniers. Saunière, for no explained reason, obliterated the inscription, but did not realize that it had been copied elsewhere. He thereafter developed the habit of wandering around the countryside with his housekeeper, Marie Denarnaud, collecting stones and rocks. He was also in correspondence with various unknown people all over the world and spent a large amount of money on postage.

Needless to say, this was abnormal behavior for a humble priest in the French countryside. He was extravagant in many other ways too. Nowadays there is a well-paved road leading up the mountain to the village, but in those days a simple dirt track would have been sufficient for the villagers' needs. Saunière, however, paid for a road to be built leading to the village. He also paid for a tower – the Tower of Magdala – to be built on the very edge of the mountain. One of the windows in the Tower is long and slender and the bricks around it form a Cross of Lorraine.

A new mansion was built – Villa Bethania – which Saunière never occupied. Lazarus and his sister Mary (who some believe to be synonymous with the Magdalene) came from Bethany and this was also the name that the Priory of Sion had given its "arch" at Rennes-le-Château.

Saunière's most significant changes took place in the church itself, which was decorated in an opulently bizarre way. Over the porch entrance was placed the inscription: "TERRIBILIS EST LOCUS ISTE," which translates as: "THIS PLACE IS TERRIBLE." Tracy Twyman explains in Dagobert's Revenge magazine that:

> ...this is a quote from Genesis, in which Jacob falls asleep on a stone and has a vision of a ladder leading up to heaven, with angels ascending and descending upon it. This, of course, is the same Stone of Destiny brought to Scotland by Joseph of Arimathea, and became the stone upon which British monarchy are crowned, even today. What's noteworthy is that beneath the words "This Place is Terrible" is etched the rest of Jacob's statement in Genesis: "...This is none but the House of God and the Gateway to Heaven," making it not a curse, but a comment upon the dual nature of divinity.

Immediately inside the entrance to the church, Saunière placed a statue of the demon Asmodeus. This is hardly what you would expect to welcome you when you enter a church. Traditionally, he is in charge of secrets, guardian of hidden treasure and according to Judaic tradition, the builder of the Temple of Solomon. He was known as "the Destroyer" as well as "Rex Mundi," a Cathar term meaning "Lord of the Earth."

Inside the church, brightly painted Stations of the Cross were placed on the walls and in some there are inconsistencies. For example, Station XIV depicts Jesus' body being carried at night under a full moon in the vicinity of a tomb. It could mean that his body was being carried to the tomb at night, several hours after the Bible would have us believe. It could, however, mean that the body is being carried out of the tomb instead, perhaps because Christ was actually alive.

Elsewhere in the church, two statues of Christ can be found just a few feet apart from each other, one slightly above the other. They are not identical. Both are pointing upwards, and the upper one appears to be pointing up towards a cupola on the wall above him, at the top of which is the rosy cross. The lower one holds the Papal authority in his hand and is surrounded by disciples. The upper Christ is pointing downwards, directly at the lower one. Perhaps this suggests an alternate Christian tradition above that of ortho-dox Christianity.

On either side of the altar are statues of Mary and Joseph, who are each shown carrying a Christ child. Could one of the children be the disciple of Christ, Thomas Didymus, who is thought to be Christ's twin? The words "Thomas" and "Didymus" both mean "twin."

Along the wall there are statues of five saints whose initials spell out G.R.A.A.L. (as in Holy Grail) – St. Germain, St. Roch, St. Anthony de Padoue, St. Anthony the Hermit and St. Luke are all placed in the shape of an "M." This "M" has been supposed to stand for "Magdalene," the patron saint of the church and matriarch of the Grail family whose legend is so important to the Priory of Sion.

The predominant motif throughout the church is the Rosy Cross. The symbol of the fleur-de-lys, the former royal arms of France, occurs everywhere too. This strengthens the evi-dence of a link between a Grail family and the French royal family. Reference is also made for the first time in *Dagobert's Revenge* by Tracy Twyman that "the church wall featured the telltale marking, a yellow stripe embedded in the founda-tion, which was used in those days to indicate that someone of royal blood was buried inside the church."

Even after completing his renovations, Saunière continued to spend. He had a magnificent library installed in the Magdala Tower. He built an orangery and a zoological gar-den and accumulated valuable collections of china, fabrics and antiques. His parishioners were treated to huge ban-quets and received visits from various well-connected fig-ures. The most noteworthy of his visitors was Archduke

Johann von Habsburg, a cousin of Franz-Josef, emperor of Austria. According to banking records, the Archduke paid Saunière considerable amounts of money.

The number 22 occurs with more than reasonable coincidence in connection with Saunière's renovations. It was, in fact, one of Saunière's secret codes. There are 22 steps leading to the roof of the Magdala Tower, which has 22 merlons circling its top. Underneath the "Glass Tower" there are 22 more steps which go down to an inaccessible basement. There are two sets of 11 steps that lead into the garden. The Templar and Masonic symbol of a Skull and Crossbones placed above the gate to the graveyard has 22 teeth. There are inscriptions in the church that have been deliberately misspelled so that they will contain 22 letters. No suitable explanation has been given for this, but there are 22 cards in the Major Arcana of the Tarot and 22 letters in the mystical Hebrew alphabet.

Although the church turned a blind eye to these goings-on, it reached a point where the Bishop of Carcassonne had to act and he summoned Saunière to make an account of himself and his dealings. He accused Saunière of simony, that is, the selling of masses. Saunière flatly refused to reveal anything and the Bishop therefore suspended him. Saunière appealed to the Vatican and he was re-instated. Then on January 17, 1917, at the age of 65, Saunière had a sudden stroke. The date is of interest. It is the same date as the death of Marie, Marquise d'Hautpol de Blanchefort, whose tomb inscription Saunière had obliterated. It is also the feast day of Saint Sulpice, who crops up again and again in this account and figures prominently in *The Da Vinci Code*.

It is said that Saunière acted against the instructions of the Priory of Sion in late 1916. Of particular significance, perhaps, is that ten days before his death, on January 12th, Saunière appeared to his parishioners to be in good health. But this was the day that his housekeeper, Marie Denarnaud, ordered his coffin. The priest who heard Saunière's deathbed confession, according to some, "never smiled again" and he refused to give Saunière the traditional Roman Catholic last rite of Extreme Unction. Saunière died on January 22nd. His body was sat upright in an armchair on the terrace of the Magdala Tower. He was dressed in an ornate robe with scarlet tassels attached. Mourners, who have never been identified, walked past his body and took tassels from the robe. No one has ever been able to explain this odd procedure. To the astonishment of everyone when the will was read, Saunière was discovered to have died penniless. Shortly before his death he transferred all of his money to his housekeeper. It is possible that she had been in charge of the money all along.

After the Second World War, the French government introduced a new currency and all citizens were obliged to exchange their old francs for the new ones. Large amounts of money had to be accounted for in order to trace "black" money saved by collaborators, tax-evaders and the like. Marie Denarnaud would not reveal the source of her money and was to be seen later burning large amounts of cash in the garden of the Villa Bethania. She eventually sold the house to Monsieur Noël Corbu and lived off the proceeds for the rest of her life. She told him that before she died she would tell him a great "secret" which would make him rich and "powerful." Unfortunately, much to the chagrin of Monsieur Corbu, on January 29, 1953, she, like Saunière, suffered a sudden stroke and was rendered speechless and prostate on her deathbed.

The Source of Saunière's Wealth

The obvious question that springs to mind is: Where did Saunière's money come from? The village and the surrounding area had been the center of considerable activity from the time that the Celts designated it to be a sacred site to the time when the Cathars were persecuted in the eleventh century. There had been tales of hidden treasure throughout this time and the Cathars especially were suspected of being the possessors of the "Holy Grail." The Knights Templar also were thought to have hidden treasure in the area and Bertrand de Blanchefort organized excavations there. The

Merovingian kings ruled much of modern France from the fifth to the eighth centuries and Dagobert II, who was one of them, married a Visigoth princess. Rennes-le-Château was at that time one of the major centers of the Visigoths. The Visigoths themselves had considerable treasure accumulated from their pillaging of Europe and in particular most of the wealth of Rome in 410 AD Saunière could have discovered any of these but the nature of his treasure appears to be more that of a secret. This explains certain factors such as the introduction he received to the Parisian intelligentsia from Hoffet and the intense interest that the church took in the matter. It also may explain why the priest refused to give Saunière the sacrament of Extreme Unction, and why he was visited by, for example, the Archduke Johann Salvator von Habsburg.[6] Treasure of mere monetary worth would also not explain the codes in the parchments and on the tomb of Marie, Marquise d'Hautpol de Blanchefort. Marie Denarnaud said that the secret she took with her to the grave involved not only money, but "power." The money that Johann Salvator von Habsburg paid over to Saunière perhaps came from another source. The Vatican treated Saunière very carefully in the latter years of his life. Could it be that the money came from the Vatican in order to silence him?

The Mystery Deepens
When *Holy Blood, Holy Grail* first came out the authors received a letter from a retired Anglican priest who claimed that he had "incontrovertible truth" that Jesus Christ did not die on the cross and could have lived to as late a date as 45 AD. On being interviewed he claimed that he had been told the information by another Anglican priest, Canon Alfred Leslie Lilley. Throughout his life, Lilley had maintained contact with the Catholic Modernist Movement that was based at Saint Sulpice in Paris and he had known Émile Hoffet. The authors felt that this connection added authenticity to his claim.

Nicolas Poussin, the previously mentioned French painter, also appears to have been privy to this secret. He was visit-

---

[6] The archduke renounced rights to his titles in 1889 and was banished from the Austrian Empire.

ed in Rome by Abbé Louis Fouquet, the brother of Nicholas Fouquet, the Financial Superintendent to Louis XIV of France, in 1656. After the meeting the Abbé wrote to his brother. Part of the letter reads: "He and I discussed certain things, which I shall with ease be able to explain to you in detail – things that will give you, through Monsieur Poussin, advantages which even kings would have great pains to draw from him, and which, according to him, it is possible that nobody else will ever be able to rediscover in the centuries to come. And, what is more, these are things so difficult to discover that nothing now on this earth can prove of better fortune nor be their equal." Nobody has been able to explain the rather cryptic message in this letter, but the fact is that shortly after receiving this letter, Nicholas Fouquet was imprisoned for life in solitary confinement. It has been suggested that he was the model for "The Man in the Iron Mask." All his correspondence was confiscated, and handed over to Louis XIV, who read it only in private. Louis XIV went to great lengths to buy Poussin's painting, *Les Bergers d'Arcadie*, which he had hidden away in his private apartments at Versailles.

You will recall that it was a copy of this painting which Berenger Saunière bought at the Louvre during his visit to Paris. The painting depicts a large ancient tomb, with three shepherds and a shepherdess in the foreground. The setting is of a rugged landscape that is typical of Poussin. The inscription on the tomb reads: "ET IN ARCADIA EGO." The landscape had long been assumed to be a product of the artist's mind. However, in the 1970s, an actual tomb was located which was identical in shape, dimensions, vegetation, background and setting. There is even a rocky outcrop that is identical to the one upon which one of the shepherds rests his foot. If you stand just in front of the tomb you will see that the view is exactly the same as the one in Poussin's painting. The corresponding peak in the background is that of Rennes-le-Château. The tomb is located just outside a village called Arques, six miles from Rennes-le-Château and three miles from the château of the Blanchefort family. There is no indication of the age of the tomb. The village records state that the land surrounding the tomb belonged to an American, who opened the sepulcher in the 1920s and found it to be empty. He died in the 1950s, and was later buried in it with his wife. This brings us back to the inscription on the tomb in Poussin's painting. It appears not to make much sense, as it lacks a verb. "Et in Arcadia Ego" translates to "And in Arcadia I..." However, an anagram of the inscription reads "I TEGO ARCANA DEI," which means: "BEGONE! I BEHOLD THE SECRETS OF GOD." Perhaps the mayor of Rennes-le-Château was correct when he said to the editors of *Dagobert's Revenge*, "This place is the center point of the world."

Sacred Geometry

Dan Brown rightly emphasizes the importance of the symbol of the pentagram in *The DaVinci Code*. In the 1970s, Henry Lincoln discovered an almost mathematically perfect pentagram shaped out of the five mountain peaks which surround Rennes-le-Château. Other monuments such as churches and châteaux throughout the Aude Valley around the village also created perfect mathematical geometry, forming a network of pentagrams and hexagrams made with even measurements of the "Megalithic Yard." This was the measurement used when such megalithic monuments as Stonehenge were constructed in prehistory. This geometry appeared to have been put there by someone quite deliberately. Lincoln's investigations into these mysteries have so far resulted in two books, *The Holy Place*, and *Key to the Sacred Pattern*, as well as two video documentaries, *The Secret: Investigating the Rennes-le-Château Mystery with Henry Lincoln* and *Henry Lincoln's Guide to Rennes-le-Château and the Aude Valley*, both distributed by Illuminated Word. Another book, *The Templars' Secret Island*, was co-written by Erling Haagensen, and deals with a similar pattern of geometry found on the Danish island of Bornholm.

When asked in an interview with *Dagobert's Revenge* magazine how he thought this geometry could possibly occur, Henry Lincoln said that at some point in ancient history someone noticed the pentagonal configuration of the mountains, deemed it to be holy, and then constructed the rest of the geometry around it. He went on to say this:

> It is not beyond the capability of homo sapiens actually to construct an artificial high point in order to perfect the geometry. You only have to look at the size of Silbury Hill, for instance, which we all know is man-made, or the Great Pyramid. So it is possible that the actual high spots which indicate the pentagon of mountains could have been refined, as it were, though I think that the original mountains in their natural state were already sufficiently close for it to be astronomically unlikely to have originated by chance. But it did. Then around that natural formation, people began to construct a geometric layout. A thousand years later, perhaps, we eventually come to that later period, in the twelfth century, when the geometry is now being laid out in the Baltic. And there it is very consciously done, and with much, much more precision. It's a development of what was begun at Rennes-le-Château and is now extended at Bornholm.

The figure that is projected by the mountains surrounding Rennes-le-Château is a perfect pentagram – the same figure that is traced out by the orbit of Venus every four years. Venus is personified by the Magdalene, to whom the church at Rennes-le-Château is dedicated.

In the same interview, Lincoln repudiates the Priory of Sion as a reliable source of information, going so far as to deny the validity of the information that he has presented in *Holy Blood, Holy Grail* and *The Messianic Legacy*: "The Priory of Sion I know nothing whatsoever about. It is purely hearsay. We don't know whether it ever existed in the form which Mr. Plantard suggested, or not. We only have their words for it.... I don't know who the Priory are."

Lincoln states that the only reliable aspect of whole subject is the geographical geometry which surrounds Rennes-le-Château and he was led to this discovery by the geometry hidden in the parchments of which the Priory of Sion were custodians.

It is also difficult to dismiss the theory that there is a link between the Judaic Davidic line and the Merovingians. The evidence for this connection throughout history is too strong to ignore. The Priory of Sion has claimed to be the factor that has kept these theories together. Furthermore, according to the Priory of Sion's own literature, their secrets originated not with Christ, but in an area we have not looked at – the antediluvian world. This is the same conclusion that other respected researchers into the mystery of Rennes-le-Château have reached.

It is possible that Baigent, Leigh and Lincoln were acting as the spokesmen for the Priory of Sion when they wrote *Holy Blood, Holy Grail* and *The Messianic Legacy*. Now that this relationship has been severed, the messenger may have turned on his employer.

Whatever the case, Henry Lincoln gave another interview after this one which thickens the mystery. In an ABC News special *Primetime Monday*, Lincoln told host Elizabeth Vargas something quite different. The transcript reads as follows:

> *Vargas: So the first Merovingian queen was impregnated by a sea creature, a fish, which you theorize could symbolize Jesus. So the Merovingian bloodline would be descendants of Jesus.*
>
> Lincoln: Mmm hmm.
>
> *Vargas: ...and this bloodline was threatened by the Orthodox Church...*
>
> Lincoln: Mmm hmm.
>
> *Vargas: ...so the Priory of Sion was established to protect this bloodline, the Merovingian bloodline.*
>
> Lincoln: Beautiful. That's very good. You've done it.

Clearly, the truly enigmatic nature of the mystery of Rennes-le-Château is impossible for even a hardened skeptic like Lincoln to ignore.

Chapter Five
Constantine the Great

CONSTANTINE THE GREAT IS CONSIDERED BY PRESENT-DAY CHRISTIANS TO BE THE INTERMEDIARY BETWEEN THE DARK PAGAN AND HERETICAL PAST AND THE ENLIGHT-ENED CIVILIZED CHRISTIAN ERA. THE RECEIVED HISTORY IS AWASH WITH MISCONCEPTIONS. ONE THING THAT IS TRUE IS THAT CONSTANTINE WAS WELL DISPOSED TOWARDS CHRISTIANS, AS HIS FATHER HAD BEEN.

In addition to being the person who first brought Christianity to Rome, Constantine was the chief priest of the state religion, Sol Invictus (the Invincible Sun) which involved sun worship, as Dan Brown relates in *The Da Vinci Code*. At that time there was another sun-worshiping cult that was popular in Rome – Mithraism. It also promoted a belief in the immortality of the soul, Judgment Day, and the resurrection of the dead. Both Sol Invictus and Mithraism, like Christianity, worshipped only one god. Sol Invictus had originated in Syria and had come to Rome about 100 years before. Constantine saw a perfect opportunity to blend the three together, achieving the political and religious unity that he saw as being vital to his own success. Conveniently, Sol Invictus, Mithraism and Christianity were similar enough from various points of view to become one.

Constantine lived in a time when political success resulted from religious piety, so despite his undoubted devotion to Christianity, there was a pragmatic reason for Constantine's favoring the religion. The number of Christians in Rome was growing and Constantine looked upon them as good support in his struggle to keep the imperial throne from his rival and brother-in-law, Maxentius. When Constantine beat him at the Battle of Milvian Bridge, just outside Rome, in 312 AD, the problem was resolved. According to the fourth century bishop and historian Eusebius of Caesarea, Constantine had had a vision before the battle in which he had seen a luminous cross hanging in the sky with the legend *In Hoc Signo Vinces*, meaning "In this sign, conquer." We are told that Constantine then ordered the Greek letter *Chi Rho*, which was the Christian monogram, to be displayed upon the shields of his troops. Because of this vision, his victory was seen to be a victory of Christianity over Paganism. Constantine thus became Emperor in the West and he ruled jointly with Licinius in the East. One of the first things he did was order that the nails from Christ's crucifixion be brought to him and he had one of them attached to his crown. He met with Licinius shortly after his victory against Maxentius and in the "Edict of Milan" which resulted, they agreed that there should be toleration of Christians and that the property that had been confiscated from them would be restored. Constantine would go on to defeat Licinius and rename Byzantium "Constantinople," the present day Istanbul in Turkey. By 313 he had donated the Lateran Palace to the Bishop of Rome, where a new cathedral was built, the Basilica Constantiniana, now S. Giovanni in Laterano.

From this point onwards, Christianity became acceptable. Contrary to tradition, Constantine chose an associate of his, Sylvester, to be the next Pope and the practice of Emperors selecting Popes was to continue. This also marked the end of the persecution of Christians. They could now live openly and worship freely. However, many felt an atmosphere of such opulence ran counter to the teachings of Christ and that the Church had been thrown badly off course. Some Christians therefore felt that Christianity had been sacrificed for the purpose of maintaining Constantine's success. As if to validate their doubts, Constantine confirmed his sacred status by proclaiming that the Christian God was his sponsor. By bringing together Christianity, Sol Invictus, Mithraism and certain elements from Syria and Persia, Constantine had indeed created a universal ("catholic") and hybrid religion.

The vision he had, in fact, took place in a Pagan temple and it was of the sun god, Sol Invictus. He had been accepted into the cult of Sol Invictus shortly before. After the victory at Milvan Bridge, the triumphal arch of Constantine was erected in Rome which states that the victory was won through the intervention of the Deity, referring not to the Christian god, but to Sol Invictus.

According to the historian Eusebius, the Desposyni, who were descendants of Jesus' family, if not his actual descendants, sent a delegation to Pope Sylvester in 318 AD. They stated that various bishoprics should be given to them, that the Mother Church should be considered to be their own Desposyni Church in Jerusalem and that the Church of Rome should continue to make financial contributions to it. Pope Sylvester rejected their demands, saying that salvation was a matter for Constantine and not Jesus Christ. This rather frosty encounter seems to have been the last time that the former Nazarean tradition had any communication with the Church of Rome that was by then committed to following the Pauline tradition.

In 321 AD, Constantine declared that the law courts should no longer close on the Jewish Sabbath, but on the "venerable day of the sun" – Sunday. In this way, Christians changed their day of rest from Saturdays to Sundays and increased the distance between Judaism and Christianity. Additionally, the birth of Christ had been celebrated traditionally until this time on January 6. This date is still important in parts of Europe as "Kings' Day." However, Christianity adopted the Sol Invictus and Mithraic festival of December 25 instead as the traditional birth date of Jesus Christ. This festival celebrated the rebirth of the sun, the resulting lengthening of the days and the sun's influence on the world. Therefore all sects celebrated together on the same day. Conveniently Mithraism also believed in other important tenets of Christian belief such as life after death and the immortality of the soul. It was now expedient for Jesus Christ to represent the Sol Invictus at the same time that Christian churches were being built. Statues of Sol Invictus were also created, bearing a resemblance to Constantine. By promoting himself, Constantine effectively demoted Jesus.

So that was Christmas dealt with. However it was not until the Council of Nicaea in 325 AD that the dating system of Easter was decided, by committee voting, to be the first Sunday after the first full moon following the northern vernal equinox (March 21). They could not agree on a specific date. The Christian festival replaced the old Pagan festival which went by the name of Eastre, the name of the goddess associated with spring, and who was also responsible for the origin of our word for the female hormone, estrogen.

The Council of Nicaea was the first ecumenical council of the Christian Church and met in ancient Nicaea, which is now Iznik in Turkey. Dan Brown ignores the main reason the Council was formed: to solve the heresy problem that had arisen because of the Arian belief in the Eastern Church that Christ was not divine, but a human being. The Council decided, again by a vote, that Jesus Christ was a god, not a man. This was of particular value to Constantine in his constant striving for unity, as Jesus Christ as a god could be associated directly with Sol Invictus. Under this new arrangement, Jesus Christ would be the mortal representative of Sol Invictus in case any awkward questions were asked. Pope Sylvester did not attend the Council, but sent representatives. Constantine himself exiled Arius, thereby emphasizing his prominence in ecclesiastical matters.

The Pauline Christians were still expecting the Second Coming of their Messiah and Constantine had to find a way to deal with this. Concentrating on the fact that Jesus Christ had failed in his mission to get the Romans out of Jerusalem, Constantine started to sow seeds of doubt that Christ had ever been the Messiah. He pointed out that it was Constantine and not Christ who had brought about the acceptance of Christians. Surely, therefore, it was he who was the Messiah? Christians who chose to hang on to the disproved idea that Jesus Christ was a Messiah were written off as heretics.

It has to be understood that Jesus, as a devout Jew, would have recoiled from the idea of creating a new religion separate from Judaism and regarded it as heresy. As we will see in Chapter Seven concerning the facts and fiction of Jesus Christ, there was a split in the Christian Church about 25 years after Christ's death between James, the brother of Christ, and St. Paul.

In order to maintain this status quo, Constantine ordered the destruction of all works that contradicted this new religion, including all writings about Jesus Christ by Pagan writers and even Christian writers who lacked the "foresight" of how history was to be rewritten. This was conducted with efficient zeal with nearly all Christian documents, especially those in Rome, disappearing to make way for their replacements. In 331 AD, Constantine seized the opportunity of conducting this whitewashing of history and ordered new versions of the New Testament to be written. The writers were free to say whatever their Christian masters thought appropriate.

What this means is the New Testament that we have today was rewritten in the fourth century with a political spin that was desirable for Constantine at the time. It is as if a US President had Shakespeare rewritten to fit in with his political agenda.

Constantine went further than this. The awaiting of the Messiah was a major part of Judaic religious tradition and the deification of monarchs has also appeared in other civilizations such as Egyptian and Roman. This person would have healing powers and correct the ills of the world. This applies, of course, not only to our received reputation of Christ, but also that of the Merovingians. For Constantine, however, the Christian god was no more than another perspective on the familiar Sol Invictus. The role he saw for himself was that of Messiah. He considered that Christ had attempted – and failed – to be what was expected of him: a person who was warrior, spiritual leader, and a unifier of politics, religion and territory. In other words, someone like

Constantine himself. And he considered that he could do the job a lot better.

Surprisingly, the Roman Church did not object to this perception. Perhaps it was aware of the fact that his mother, Helena, the British Princess Elaine of Camulod, the daughter of King Coel II, was of Arimathean descent and therefore of genuine Grail extraction. Constantine could therefore justify his elevated position through the Merovingian bloodline. The church was also ready to acknowledge that the purpose of a Messiah was not to be that of a benign humanitarian savior, but a forceful, strong, militant leader. From this point onwards, the founder of Christianity as we know it is not Jesus Christ of the first century, but Constantine the Great of the fourth. Eusebius was also convinced of Constantine's quasi-divinity and his additional belief that he was effectively the thirteenth apostle.

However, this smokescreen is as nothing compared to the Donation of Constantine and the effects and repercussions that it has had on all of us in the western world, Christian or not, since its "discovery."

Constantine was not baptized as a Christian until he was dying in 337. He wanted to be baptized in the river Jordan but circumstances did not allow this. For the baptism he took off his purple imperial robes and wore the white garments of the neophyte.

The Donation of Constantine
Once Constantine was made Holy Roman Emperor, he clearly had the world at his feet, in every sense of the word. A document appeared in the eighth century called the *Donation of Constantine*. This meant it was supposedly four hundred years before it was found. Considering its implications, it is odd that it was not found sooner. Its purpose was to confirm that the Popes were God's representatives on earth. But that was not all.

The Roman Church claimed that it had been written in the fourth century, presumably before Constantine's death in 337 AD, as a result of the gratitude that Emperor

Constantine the Great had to Pope Sylvester for curing him of leprosy. In recognition and acknowledgement of his thanks, he transferred the entire power of the Holy Roman Empire to the Church. This included the right to select and deselect monarchs.

The Roman Church set to work immediately, implementing it in 751 AD when they made Pepin the First King of France. This is when the Merovingian kings were first deposed by the Church and replaced by their servants, the Mayors of the Palace. The Church offered to support the ensuing Roman Catholic puppet monarchs, the Carolingians. There can be little doubt that the Merovingians would have been suspicious of this document. After all, Constantine was of the same blood as them and they could only marvel at his idiocy at having signed away their centuries of birthright. We are also expected to believe that Constantine signed away all his robes and royal regalia, but the Pope, being a gentleman, refused to accept them.

This was the Church's way of usurping the rightful Royal bloodline for itself. From the public's point of view, the rights were Constantine's to give as he saw fit.

From that time the Church of Rome has risen with meteoric force. Every European monarch has been in power as a result of coronations conducted by the Church's representatives. All laws in monarchies that have been passed by their governments have existed by virtue of this document. The Church's power was therefore absolute.

The problem was, however, that the *Donation of Constantine* was a fraud and the Church has never legitimately had the power to wield such rights. This is a known fact since Lorenzo Valla tested its authenticity during the Renaissance. He found that the New Testament wording in the references that appear in the *Donation* came from the Vulgate version of the Bible and had not existed before. This version had been compiled by St. Jerome, who was not born until about twenty years after Constantine was supposed to have signed the *Donation*.

Furthermore, the Latin in which it is written, Pig Latin, was not in use until the eighth century. The Latin that was used in the fourth century was classical. Also the ceremonies that are mentioned in the Donation did not exist in Constantine's day. However, this has not stopped arguably the biggest fraud in history, the Donation, being used to this very day!

The Church wasted no opportunity to assert its authority in the Middle Ages on the back of this lie. A letter from Pope Gregory IX to Emperor Frederick II entitled "Si Memorium Beneficiorum," dated October 23, 1236, says:

> .... that as the Vicar of the Prince of Apostles (the Roman Pope) governed the empire of priesthood and of souls in the whole world so he should also reign over things and bodies throughout the whole world; and considering that he should rule over earthly matters by the reins of justice to whom — as it is known — God had committed on earth the charge over spiritual things. The Emperor Constantine humbled himself by his own vow and handed over the empire to the perpetual care of the Roman Pontiff with the Imperial Insignia and scepters and the City and Duchy of Rome...

In Britain, through application of the Donation, coronations have been performed, wrongly, by Archbishops of the Church of England. When Henry VIII split from the Roman Catholic church because of his marriage requirement, he retained the right of Archbishops to create monarchs through coronation and thereby perpetuated the fraud through every British monarch since. Of course, he should not have been there in the first place anyway. As we know from the parentage of Edward IV covered in Chapter Three regarding the Bloodline, no Tudor should have even glimpsed the throne.

If we take the matter to its logical conclusion, the implications of this fraud are enormous: All laws that have been passed in Britain and ratified by monarchs who have been wrongly crowned by Archbishops as a result of the Donation of Constantine are invalid.

Chapter Six
The Holy Grail in Europe

IN CHAPTER THREE WE CONCENTRATED ON THE INTER-
PRETATION OF THE HOLY GRAIL AS A SYMBOL FOR THE
DESCENDANTS OF CHRIST THROUGH HIS WIFE, MARY
MAGDALENE. WE HAVE EXPLAINED AT LENGTH THEIR ROLE
IN PROVIDING THE BLOODLINE OF THE ROYAL FAMILIES
OF EUROPE. DAN BROWN SPENDS MUCH TIME ON THIS
THEORY IN *THE DA VINCI CODE*. HOWEVER, THERE IS ALSO
A BELIEF THAT THE HOLY GRAIL IS ACTUALLY A VESSEL OF
SOME SORT AND SO THERE ARE POSSIBLY AT LEAST TWO
REAL "HOLY GRAILS" TO CONTEMPLATE.

When the Celts arrived in Western Europe, having traveled
across the Alps and central Europe, they brought with them not
only iron, but the horse. One of their customs was to throw
their swords (to which they attributed magical powers), along
with bits of jewelry, into what they perceived to be sacred lakes.
As King Arthur lay dying, one of his closest followers is said to
have thrown his sword, Excalibur, into such a lake in accordance with Celtic tradition. Lakes were believed to be the
entrance to the underworld, the kingdom of the Dead, which
was thought to be situated at the center of the earth. Arthur is
said to have died on the island of Avalon. It is not clear where
Avalon was. Some say it was at Michael's Mount off the southern English coast, others at Mont St. Michel off the French
coast. The area around Glastonbury is also thought to have been
the possible location, as legend has it that Arthur is buried
there. The name "Avalon" is associated with apples, and
Excalibur is said to have been forged at Glastonbury.

Excalibur served King Arthur well; it could defeat any foe
and it is said that Arthur became King only because he was

able to take Excalibur from the stone in which it was fixed. Others say that this story refers allegorically to Arthur's ability to extract iron from rock which was one of the skills that the Celts brought with them.

In addition to sacred swords, there are many ancient traditions regarding sacred vessels, such as the "Horn of Plenty," which could purportedly provide a never-ending supply of food and comfort. This notion must have been appealing to those living in often hunger-stricken times. Many containers such as bowls, jugs, chalices and cauldrons were considered to have supernatural powers. Similarly the Grail was thought to bring nourishment and salvation.

According to a Celtic tradition, King Arthur and his men engaged themselves in a quest for a magical cauldron. It was not until the Middle Ages that the story was removed from its Pagan background and given a Christian significance. Arthur was a popular king, believed to be the only person who could defeat the invading Scots after the departure of the Romans in the fifth century, and he heralded a long period of calm prosperity afterwards. In his time, Christianity was taking hold in a Britain still heavily influenced by Paganism. Legends from this time have both Pagan and Christian influences.

The Celts believed that nature was divine and that everything within it communicated with man. The countryside was alive with fairies and elves who mapped out man's fortunes. The good were rewarded, the bad punished. Warriors were believed to be resurrected at Judgment Day unless they had been beheaded, which was the typical fate of enemies captured.

One of the most common rituals in the Christian religion is communion in which the blood of Christ, represented by wine, is drunk. The basis of the Arthurian version of the legend is the story that the Roman captain, Longinus, pierced the side of Christ when he was crucified to make sure that he was dead. Then Joseph of Arimathea collected the blood in the same chalice that Christ had used for the wine at the Last Supper. This chalice is generally thought to be the Holy Grail. The corpse of Christ was then said to be put into the family vault of Joseph of Arimathea. Upon the return of the English soldiers from Palestine to England in 1274, after the nearly-failed Crusade of Edward I, English morale needed a boost. King Arthur's knights were depicted as simple warriors in search of a cause. The quest for the Holy Grail fulfilled this purpose perfectly.

As Joseph of Arimathea was a follower of Christ, he was imprisoned by the Romans shortly after the Crucifixion. He is supposed to have kept the chalice, and to have taken it with him on his journeys to Rome and the south of France, where he lived for some time in the Languedoc province with Mary Magdalene and some of the other disciples. He (possibly along with the Christ himself) is thought to have then gone to England where he spent the rest of his life in what is now the southern English town of Glastonbury. The first Christian church in Britain was founded there, on the spot where the present ruins of the abbey now stand and where the Holy Grail was perhaps kept. It was then lost and the quest by King Arthur and his knights to find it started from this point.

Arthur's quest for the Holy Grail is thought to have started at a lake (where he intended to enter the underworld) near Camelot, if, indeed, Camelot existed. He was initially denied entry, but managed to persuade the various ghosts and demons to let him in. He then managed to take the vessel from them. If it did exist, it would have been taken to Arthur's headquarters, which would most likely have been a collection of rough wooden huts, lacking the palatial grandeur of the Hollywood version. It could have been in any one of several possible locations. One of the most likely is the hill-fort of Cadbury in Somerset in southern England, where there was a large fifth century settlement.

It was not until the eleventh century, 500 years after Arthur's death, that interest in him and his knights started. By tradition they conformed to the qualities of chivalry and honor in creating a classless utopian society. It was an age of right-eousness in which communication with the supernatural was thought to be possible. King Arthur and his knights served as a reminder of Christ and his disciples. The Arthurian court was, however, torn apart by the love that Lancelot had for Arthur's wife, Guinevere. She was condemned to death and Lancelot banished. Lancelot was eventually overcome by remorse and joined a monastery, where he lived for the rest of his life.

The Middle Ages was a period of great piety and this was when the age of the pilgrimage started. One of the present-day major Christian pilgrimages to Santiago de Compostela started at this time and there are many small churches on the route that was (and still is) used. In about 1200 the Catholic Church accepted the idea of Transubstantiation — that is, the turning of wine into the actual blood of Christ. Chrétien of Troy wrote his Grail romances at this time, creating a Christian story from a Pagan concept.

Not everyone agreed with the way that the Catholic Church was developing. The Cathars, advocating a life of poverty and simplicity, rejected the opulence that was characteristic of the Church at that time. In true Dan Brown-style coding, they preferred to think of their Church as AMOR ("Love") rather than ROMA ("Rome"). The Pope launched a persecution of the Cathars and they were besieged at Montsegur in southern France, where it is thought that they kept the Grail, among other treasures, although there is no clear evidence to suggest this. They managed to have it all smuggled out before the two week siege, which ended with many of them being burned alive.

It is believed that the Holy Grail was kept in Italy for 300 years, where it was guarded by the monk St. Lawrence, deacon of the Church of Rome. He is thought to have had it taken by two Spanish legionaries to his home town of Huesca in the Spanish Pyrenees towards the end of the third century. His life ended unpleasantly — he was roasted on a gridiron a few days after his friend Pope Sixtus II was executed. The Grail was kept at the church of San Pedro el Viejo until 711. There are several examples of Grail imagery in the Romanesque cloister, including an angel passing a cup to Jesus.

Wolfram von Eschenbach, who died in 1230, is generally considered to be the greatest of the medieval German narrative poets. One of his major works was *Perceval*, which was later the subject of the opera by Richard Wagner. One of his main sources was Chrétien's work, written in conjunction with other material that Wolfram claims was provided by Kyot of Provence. Kyot may have based his stories on those that he had heard in Spain, where there were both Muslim and Jewish philosophers, and in Toledo in particular which was a center of science and literature at this time. Wolfram maintained that the Grail was a stone which had magical powers and, like the Horn of Plenty, offered a constant supply of food and eternal youth.

King Alfonso I of Aragón and Navarra used to go to San Pedro el Viejo in Huesco for contemplation. The name Alfonso is closely related to the Latin name Anfortius, and is clearly connected to the Grail story King, Anfortus. It is probable, therefore, that Alfonso was the model for the Grail King. At the end of his life he retreated to San Pedro el Viejo where he was fatally wounded. Likewise, in the Grail legend, the Grail King Anfortus waited at his castle for Parcival to bring him the deliverance from his wounds, but it was many years before Parcival reached the castle of Anfortus. It is likely that Alfonso's cousin, the Spanish count Perche de Val (1100 – 1144) was the model for Parcival.

The Knights Templar are reputed to have been the keepers of the Grail. The Grail castle was said to be visible only in a state of grace and otherwise hidden from sight. These are not the customary characteristics of castles, which were traditionally intended to be conspicuous, dominant and built on high ground to oversee the surrounding land. The concept of a hidden castle would have been difficult for the medieval mind to understand.

However, there is one perfectly hidden place in Spain which fits the description, and that is the monastery of San Juan de Peña. It is considered to be built on the sacred ground where the Spanish province of Aragón originated. The anchor, which was Parcival's coat of arms, is seen in the burial niches in the large courtyard. It was necessary to move the Grail from place to place in the Pyrenees because of the constant threat from the Muslims. The Monastery of San Juan de la Peña is one of these places where the Grail was kept, and it was from here that it was transferred to its present location.

There is an entry in the Royal Register in the library of Barcelona, Spain, which tells of a fortified abbey and a gift that was made to it. The gift is described by a half-Spanish, half-Latin phrase, *calice lapideum*, meaning "stone chalice" and refers to the same one that was said to be at the chapel, which is constructed like a temple, in San Juan de la Peña. The Grail would have been kept either in one of the vaults that are hewn out of the stone or else on the altar. This chapel is the room that Parcival was searching for and it is described as a chapel within a castle. The story tells us that when Parcival arrived there, he saw the procession in which the Grail Maiden carried the Grail to the Grail King. A carrier behind her brought the lance that Longinus used to pierce the side of Christ, which magically continued to bleed from its tip. Following them came a female bearer who carried the platter on which the head of John the Baptist had been presented.

Some readers may remember a book called *The Spear of Destiny* by Trevor Ravenscroft, which purports to be an historical account of the rise of Hitler to power based on his belief in the magical powers of the spear of Longinus. It is built on the premise that Longinus, who pierced the side of Jesus, held the future of the world in his hands for a brief period. Charlemagne was known to have carried this spear in battle as a lucky talisman. However, a skeptical approach to the book is advised.

The final resting place of the Holy Grail (where we may see it to this day) is in a side chapel in Valencia Cathedral in Spain. Although the Catholic Church has never acknowledged it to be a holy relic, they recognize it as the chalice that Christ blessed at the Last Supper and which was used by Popes in Rome until it was taken to Spain by St. Lawrence. It is now kept behind bullet-proof glass. The King of Navarre took the Grail to Valencia Cathedral on March 18, 1437, and it has remained there ever since, except for two brief periods when it was removed for safe-keeping during the War of Independence against France and during the Spanish Civil War.

Its pure gold base is decorated with 28 pearls, two red gem stones, and two emeralds. Its height is 5.5 cm, diameter 9.5 cm, thickness 3 mm. Including its base, it measures 17 cm by 14.5 cm. The eminent archaeologist Antonio Beltran says that the Grail as we see it today was made in San Juan de la Peña, probably by goldsmiths from Byzantium. The upper part of the chalice comes from the Near East and was made in either Alexandria or Antioch. Beltran says that it is beyond doubt that the chalice was made sometime between the latter half of the last century BC and the first half of the first century AD. This dates it precisely to the time of Christ.

Antonio Beltran explains that it is the stone base of the composition that is the actual Grail. On this part, which forms the foot of the vessel, there is an inscription in Arabic which nobody has been able to translate with complete certainty. Various interpretations include "For Him who Gives Splendor"; "Glory to Mary"; "The Merciful One" (which is how the Arabs refer to Allah); and "The Flourishing One." According to some legends the inscription LAPIS EXCILLIS appeared on it at times.

We shall perhaps never know the true identity of the Holy Grail, but this small and beautiful object, which we can actually visit today, is likely to be the actual cup used by Christ 2000 years ago which has formed the basis for so much of Western mythology and romanticism. The Holy

Grail continues to intrigue; it is part of our cultural fabric and the expression itself now has a common slang meaning denoting something which is sought after. The quest for the Holy Grail, then, involved not necessarily the discovery of the physical object itself, but identifying what the Grail is and what it means.

Chapter Seven
Jesus Christ – the facts and fiction

ABOUT 25 YEARS AFTER CHRIST'S CRUCIFIXION, A SCHISM OCCURRED IN THE MOVEMENTS THAT WERE TO FORM WHAT WE KNOW AS PRESENT-DAY CHRISTIANITY. THIS WAS A RESULT OF ST. PAUL'S VERSION OF CHRISTIANITY BECOMING THE MORE WIDELY ACCEPTED FORM OF THE RELIGION. THERE IS NOW NO TRACE OR WRITINGS OF THE OTHER FORM WHICH WAS, IN FACT, THE ONE THAT JESUS CHRIST'S FAMILY AND FRIENDS WERE MEMBERS OF.

Paul was born in Turkey. His parents were wealthy and Jewish. He also happened to be a citizen of Rome which occupied Palestine at the time. This was to prove crucial in the development and success of his version of Christianity.

The leader of the other faction, the Jesus movement, was James, who is widely believed to be the eldest of Christ's four brothers. Despite his strong relationship with Jesus, James does not appear anywhere in the New Testament during the narration of Christ's life and appears only after his death. He was as orthodox a Jew as was possible. It was said that he spent so much time praying that he developed "camel's knees." On the death of Jesus he became the head of the Jerusalem Church.

Paul was a persecutor of Christians until his vision of the risen Christ on the road to Damascus. He positioned himself to become one of the major Christian leaders. However, unlike St. Peter who was a bona fide disciple of Jesus and who was considered to have founded the Roman Catholic Church as Rome's first bishop, Paul never actually met Jesus.

Despite this, however, he was convinced that *his* views on Christianity were correct. After all, he had received his message spiritually in a vision whereas James and the rest of his family had only known Jesus personally! Paul thought that to compensate for having persecuted Christians, he would devote the rest of his life to spreading Jesus' word throughout the world.

Unfortunately his ideas conflicted seriously with those of James. They could not agree on Jesus' birth, his message and whether or not he was divine.

After Christ's death there was considerable debate on Christ's actual identity. As we saw in Chapter Five on Constantine the Great, the Arians (led by Arius) believed that he was simply a man who had been born of a woman in the normal way. For this heresy, they were eventually exiled. Jesus was not the only healer and miracle worker of his day. But it was only he who spoke of the kingdom of God. When Jesus asks Peter who he thinks Jesus is, Peter replies that Jesus is the Messiah. To Peter this meant that Jesus was the King, the one who had been anointed as had all kings who descended from the Davidic line. He recognized that Jesus' role was to liberate the Jews from the Romans and bring about a state of heaven on earth. The meaning of the word Messiah in the first century was quite specific and meant one who would defeat God's enemies and bring back God's justice. The word Messiah comes from ancient Egyptian. The Egyptians used crocodile fat, which symbolized sexual prowess, when anointing their kings. The Egyptian word for "crocodile" is *"messeh."*

James considered that Paul was destroying the good inherent in the message. Paul had allowed Gentiles (non Jews) to join his movement with no regard for Jewish law. For example, James felt that the Gentiles should observe such fundamental tenets as eating only kosher food and circumcision. They were, however, under no obligation to do so according to the doctrine promoted by Paul.

In about 50 AD, the dispute reached the point at which it had to be resolved. James and Paul met to discuss their differences. James insisted that the Gentiles should eat kosher food if they were in the presence of Jews. Paul was indignant and saw this as an outrageous encroachment on his and his followers' freedom. He referred to James and his followers as his "enemies in the Church." Eventually Paul, who comes across in all accounts as being on the hysterical side, agreed to a compromise: that the Jesus Movement would remain Jewish in principle, but non-Jews would be allowed to eat non-kosher food and not have to be circumcised.

For the next few years Paul continued delivering his message throughout the Roman Empire to the Gentiles. He promised to leave the James led faction of the movement well alone.

Then James started hearing stories about Paul.

Furious, James summoned Paul to Jerusalem in 58 AD. Paul had not been back to Jerusalem for a long time and we can imagine his apprehension of the potential danger he was in. Because of this, he had come well-prepared with a sizeable financial contribution. But this had little effect on James. He angrily dismissed Paul's offer of money, accusing him of encouraging Jews to break Jewish law as Paul had told them that they need not observe it any longer. Paul was unable to deny the charges, but he did try to assure James of his loyalty. James, rather naively, asked Paul to prove this by going to the Temple to take part in the purification ceremonies. Paul must have rubbed his hands at what appeared to be an easy way out and agreed to it immediately. Manipulative liar to the last, he freely admitted in one of his letters that he was all things to all men: "I am a Greek to the Greek, a Jew to the Jew, a law-keeper to the law-keeper, and will do whatever I have to do to win."

Other Jews were not as gullible as James and they recognized Paul's hypocrisy. They rioted in protest, and in the melee that ensued, Paul pulled out his trump card, declaring himself to be a Roman citizen. This meant the Roman soldiers were obliged to rescue him from the clutches of the angry mob.

Our perceptions of Jesus are all drawn from the information that has been passed down to us directly from this one man, Paul, and filtered through him. He influenced the writing of the four gospels with a decidedly political spin, giving the impression that there was no such thing as Jewish patriotism. Most scholars believe that the gospels emanated from the Pauline epistles in particular, and were all written after Paul's death. According to Mohd Elfie Nieshaem Juferi's essay, *The Influence of the Pauline Epistles Upon The Gospels of The New Testament: Study and Criticism*, "Paul is also claimed to be the author of the Epistles to the Romans, 1 and 2, Corinthians, Galatians, Ephesians, Philippians, Colossians, 1 and 2, Thessalonians, 1 and 2, Timothy, Titus, Philemon and Hebrews." This meant that he wrote all of the New Testament except for the gospels, which were based upon his writings.

The Romans are hardly mentioned in the gospels – odd considering that there was so much ongoing Jewish resistance against the Romans at the time. However, bear in mind that the word "gospel" means "good news" which could also be interpreted as "propaganda." Paul's intention was to create a religion that was non-Jewish, inoffensive, palatable and digestible throughout the Roman Empire.

Palestine at the time of Jesus was a boiling, angry place subjected to the evil horrors of the Roman occupation. The Romans invaded about 60 years before Jesus' birth and punished the Jewish insurrection with thousands of crucifixions. The Jews conducted a full-scale rebellion against the Romans in 66 AD, and this struggle lasted until 74 AD. At Masada, at the south-western corner of the Dead Sea, 960 Jewish men, women, and children committed suicide after holding out against the Romans long after the rest of Palestine had been crushed. The area of Galilee, where Jesus came from, was governed by Herod Antipas, a cruel and sadistic despot. The only Jews that prospered were the collaborators. The Jewish peasants lived in abject poverty and great fear. The Dead Sea scrolls that were found at Qumran in 1947 are strongly militant and indicate the desire to eradicate Romans throughout their Empire.

According to the Pauline version of history, Jesus was the son of God and not man. The real story had to be rewritten therefore, and meant that he had to be born of a virgin. Matthew wrote his gospel based upon the prophecy in the Book of Isaiah, "Behold, a virgin shall conceive and bear a child." Meanwhile, inconveniently, James, the leader of the now defunct Jerusalem Church was continuing to relate stories of his ordinary childhood with Jesus in the family home to anyone willing to listen.

The Pauline faction recognized that it was important to spread the story that Jesus was born in Bethlehem as that is where David had been born and where it had been prophesized that the next Messiah should come from. A reason had to be found for Mary and Joseph to be in Bethlehem for the birth. The New Testament tells us that Mary and Joseph had to be there as a result of there being a Roman census at that time. There is no such census on record. It is also doubtful that Jesus was from Nazareth as no records appear of a town by that name at the time. The confusion may have arisen from the name of the Nazarene or Nazarite sect of which Joseph was a member. Also, the modern Arabic word for "Christians" is Nasrani and the Christians are referred to as Nasara or Nazara.

Undoubtedly, the real Jesus Christ was a very different figure to the images that have come down to us from the Pauline camp. He was a revolutionary whose purpose was to get the Romans out of his land. His concepts of religion and politics blended together to achieve this end.

After John the Baptist was executed, Jesus recruited his own disciples. These without doubt included Mary Magdalene. She was to stand by him for the rest of his life. The Gospels say that it was she who went to Jesus' tomb to anoint him. The debate on whether she was, in fact, his wife, is covered in Chapter Eight, but we should establish now that it would only be acceptable for a wife to carry out this procedure.

Paul did not recognize that Jesus' role as King was to liberate the Jews from the Romans. To him the word "Messiah" meant that Jesus was the son of God who had come down to earth to die on the cross to redeem man. Jesus had not filled the role of Messiah as had been expected of him as he had not delivered his people from oppression, but through his resurrection he effectively redefined the term. His followers believed that only God could have been responsible for the miracle of the resurrection. This meant that the term "Messiah" adopted a characteristic of someone who was divine.

The whole Messiah issue was highly inflammatory. The Romans had abolished the Jewish monarchy and therefore anyone who even hinted at making the claim to be the Jewish King was contravening Roman law at its highest level.

Jesus entered Jerusalem on the back of an ass, as every King from the Davidic line had come to his coronation in this way from the time of King Solomon. The custom not only indicated the humility of the King, but was also a sign that he was a monarch who did not rule but served in true Messianic (later Merovingian) tradition.

Again according to tradition, Jesus entered on the day of the Passover. By following these customs, Jesus was leaving no room for doubt of his intentions. Pontius Pilate, the Roman prefect, was not the benign ruler that the New Testament would have us believe. He ruled with a merciless rod of iron and would have appreciated the potential explosiveness of the situation.

When Jesus entered the Temple and overturned the tables of the money lenders, it was not an attack on the Jews. It was the Romans who were in ultimate charge of the Temple, although it was the House of God as far as the Jews were concerned. What it represented was the center of the collaboration that occurred between the Romans and some Jews. The attack upon it was therefore an attack upon the Romans. The incident alarmed the Roman authorities who realized how the problems Jesus was causing were escalating out of control.

Another misconception that we have been fed is the supposed betrayal of Jesus by Judas. It would have been self-destructive for Judas to have done so as it would have highlighted the fact that he was a disciple of Jesus. The reason he was chosen for this role is the close association that his name has with the Jewish people who were accused of being responsible for condemning Jesus, an anti-Semitic ploy.

The New Testament tells us that Jesus was tried first by the Jewish priests for the blasphemy of calling himself the son of God. Then he was tried by the Romans for subversion and Pontius Pilate was persuaded by the Jews to execute him. In the eyes of the New Testament, it is the Jews who conspired against Jesus. That flies in the face of not only history, but logic. It was the Romans who executed their victims by crucifixion – the Jewish punishment for blasphemy, of which we are led to believe they found him guilty, was stoning. One of the purposes of crucifixion was that the bodies were left hanging to be eaten as carrion by vultures and dogs to act as a visible form of Roman justice. This also meant, of course, that tombs were neither necessary nor used. In fact, out of the many thousands of crucifixion victims in the area at that time, only one crucified skeleton has ever been found. According to the New Testament, an exception to this rule was made in Jesus' case.

The most significant aspect of Jesus' life, as far as Paul was concerned, was his death and resurrection. Therefore details of his life are scant and have not had to stand the test of time in order to uphold the Pauline tradition. On the other hand, to the Jerusalem Church, Jesus' death was a sign of failure. However, Jesus' followers believed that he was resurrected and therefore not dead. In their eyes he would continue his work of liberating them and restore the earth to the kingdom of God. There is no facility in Judaism for a human to be deemed divine.

As Paul's story gained momentum, James and the other members of the Jerusalem Church were sidelined. They developed into a small sect known as the Ebionites by the second century and were regarded as heretics.

The Pauline church is now recognized as the precursor of all the various denominations of present-day Christianity. Ironically it is a 2000 year old example of the Darwinist and "unchristian" principle of the survival of the fittest. The New Testament has not come down to us intact. Some Gospels were discarded as they did not fit in with the "official line" of Christianity. The original conflicting gospels of Matthew, Mark, Luke and John have been translated and rewritten according to the fashion and political whims of the day. There are about five thousand manuscript versions of the New Testament in existence and none of them is from earlier than the fourth century. But some still believe that although the ancient handle and blade of the Christian axe have been replaced time and time again, we are still being shown the original, when this is demonstrably untrue.

Chapter Eight
Was Jesus Married?

ONE OF THE BIGGEST QUESTIONS RAISED IN *THE DA VINCI CODE* IS WHETHER OR NOT JESUS CHRIST WAS MARRIED. HIS MARRIAGE, IN FACT, FORMS THE BASIS OF THE WHOLE MEROVINGIAN THEORY, SO IT IS CRUCIAL TO FORM AN OPINION ONE WAY OR THE OTHER.

As Dan Brown stated on the ABC News show *Primetime Monday*, nowhere in the Bible does it say that Mary Magdalene was a prostitute. The confusion has arisen through her being mentioned immediately after a story of a prostitute. The story was given credence in 591 when Pope Gregory the Great stated in his Easter sermon that Mary Magdalene and the prostitute were the same woman. This was corrected by the Vatican in 1969. Gregory the Great also stated that Mary Bethany and Mary Magdalene were the same woman.

It does not state in the Bible that Jesus was married. However, it would have almost certainly have stated the fact if *he was not*, if that were the case. It was as much a duty for a father to ensure that his son married when he reached a certain age as it was for him to ensure that he was circumcised when a baby. Furthermore there was a legal requirement for the heir to the Davidic throne to marry.

The rules that governed dynastic marriages, such as Jesus would have taken part in, differed greatly from those followed by ordinary Jewish people. The only reason that a sexual relationship was permitted to take place was to procreate. The whole marriage/sex custom was strictly regulated. Laurence Gardner goes into the subject in detail in *Bloodline* of the Holy Grail. There was a period of betrothal of three months and a First Marriage with anointing took place in September. This marked the beginning of the espousal period. However, it was not until the first half of December of the same year that a sexual relationship was allowed. This was to ensure that a baby would be born in September, the month of Atonement. If this liaison resulted in conception, the marriage was legalized by a Second Marriage which took place in the following March. If there was no conception, the sexual relationship could only resume in the following December. Until the Second Marriage, the woman was considered to be an almah. This meant "young woman," which had no sexual connotation. It is also interpreted as "virgin," meaning, obviously incorrectly in this case, "virgo intacto." At the time of the Second Marriage in March, the bride would therefore be three months pregnant. The reason for this three month delay was to allow for a possible miscarriage. It also meant that the husband could withdraw from the marriage if the woman proved herself to be infertile. Apart from the time in December when sexual relations were allowed, husbands and wives lived apart.

At the point at which they separated, the wife was referred to as a widow which was one rank below an almah. She was required to weep for her husband, described in Luke 7:38 when she "stood at his feet behind him weeping, and began to wash his feet with tears." If Christ had been conceived during this "widow" period (and it does seem that he was conceived at some point before Mary and Joseph's wedding was complete) that would make Christ the "son of a Widow." This, of course, is how Hiram Abiff is referred to in Freemasonry; what Perceval is referred to as in the Grail legends; and what Horus is referred to as in Egyptian mythology.

One of the aromatic ointments used in the marriage rites was spikenard, which is used by Mary of Bethany, otherwise known as Mary Magdalene, to anoint Jesus. She anointed his head at the house of Simon Zelotes, better know as Lazarus. In June, 30 AD, she anointed his feet with spikenard at the wedding feast at Cana.

John does not mention the actual wedding at Cana – only the feast. Among the guests were the disciples and "unclean" Gentiles. It seems clear that it was Jesus who was the bridegroom on this occasion. When the incident concerning the lack of Communion wine arose, Jesus' mother told the servants to do whatever he told them to do. It would be out of the question for a guest at a wedding to be allowed this right. The actual ceremony would take place the following September. Mary Magdalene anointed Jesus' feet again in March, 33 AD, and wiped them dry with her hair. The only person who was allowed to anoint with spikenard was a Messianic bride and the only times that it was permitted were at the First and Second Marriage ceremonies.

It was the custom of the Egyptian kings to marry their sisters. The Kings of Judah did not follow this practice but considered that the regal succession went down the female line. John the Baptist was of the Zadok male line and the wives of this line always took the title Elisheba (Elizabeth). The wives of the Davidic line, which Jesus belonged to, took the title Mary. This explains why both Jesus' mother and wife are called Mary.

In one of the Gnostic Gospels, the Gospel of Philip, which the Christian Church repressed and which The Da Vinci Code's Sir Leigh Teabing (whose name is a play on Holy Blood, Holy Grail authors Leigh and Baigent, of which Teabing is an anagram) considers to be "always a good place to start," the affection between Mary Magdalene and Jesus is described, as Dan Brown tells us:

> And the companion of the Savior is Mary Magdalene. But Christ loved her more than all the disciples, and used to kiss her often on the mouth. The rest of the disciples were offended by it and expressed disapproval. They said unto him, "why do you love her more than all of us?" The Savior answered and said to them, "Why do I not love you like her?... Great is the mystery of marriage – for without it the world would not have existed. Now the existence of the world depends on man, and the existence of man on marriage."

Kissing on the mouth was a practice reserved exclusively for those who were married. What Mr. Brown does not mention is that in the Gospel of Thomas, when Peter says "women are not worthy of life," Jesus responds, "I myself shall lead her in order to make her male... For every woman who will make herself male will enter the Kingdom of Heaven."

The Church has done everything in its power to suppress information about Christ's marriage. In 1958 a manuscript of the Ecumenical Patriarch of Constantinople was found in a monastery near Jerusalem by Morton Smith, Professor of Ancient History at Columbia University.

He discovered a letter from Bishop Clement of Alexandria (150 AD to 215 AD) to his colleague Theodore in a book of the works of St. Ignatius of Antioch. Included was part of the Gospel of Mark which had previously been unknown. He stated that this part of the Gospel should be omitted as it did not conform to the teachings of the Church. The Gospel of Mark was significant as it was the first to be written and formed the basis of all the other gospels!

The part that was repressed has Lazarus, whom Christ is said to have miraculously raised from the dead, crying out from the tomb, indicating that he was not dead when Jesus saw him. Lazarus had, in fact, been excommunicated and this was considered as being on a par with death. The period that excommunication took to complete was four days. On the third day Martha and Mary sent a message to Jesus that Lazarus was about to lose his soul to eternal damnation. Jesus was there to reinstate him even though it was technically out of his power to help. In addition, the part that was suppressed did not mention the resurrection and ends with the women running out of the empty cave. The last twelve verses of the version of Mark 16 that we have today were added at a later date.

When the arrival of Jesus at the house where Martha and Mary live is described in John, it gives the impression that Mary is hesitant to leave the house. However in the part of the Gospel of Mark that was cut out, it explains that Mary came out of the house with Martha to greet Jesus, but the disciples told her to return indoors. The reason was that as Jesus' wife, she was only permitted to leave the house with his permission.

Roman Catholics claim that St. Peter was the founder of the Catholic Church. The name Peter comes from the Greek petros, meaning stone, which was the name Christ gave to him. He had a reputation as a misogynist, or as Dan Brown would say, "a sexist," and if that is true we can understand why the Church that he was instrumental in founding has disregarded women throughout history. However, if we are to believe that Mary Magdalene was good enough not only to be Jesus' most faithful disciple, but also his wife, we have to ask ourselves such questions as why women are not allowed to be Roman Catholic priests? Furthermore, we must ask ourselves why the Church is unwilling to admit to the marriage of Christ? Given the evidence, we can only conclude, as Dan Brown does through the character of Sir Leigh Teabing, that the Christian Church wished to "declare itself the sole vessel through which humanity could access the divine and gain entrance to the kingdom of heaven."

Chapter Nine
Opus Dei

THE DA VINCI CODE, AS A DETECTIVE/ADVENTURE NOVEL, NEEDS TO REFLECT BOTH GOOD AND BAD IN AN "US" VS. "THEM" SCENARIO. WE ARE LED TO BELIEVE THAT WE SHOULD SUPPORT THE PRIORY OF SION AND ITS MEMBERS' RIGHT TO PROTECT THEIR "SECRET." HOWEVER, TO COUNTERBALANCE THIS WE ARE PRESENTED WITH OPUS DEI, A SUPPOSEDLY FANATICAL AND FABULOUSLY WEALTHY ROMAN CATHOLIC CULT CONSISTING OF INDOCTRINATED DRONES WHO CARRY OUT ITS DIRTY WORK.

A visit to the Opus Dei website (www.opusdei.org) shows priests grinning from ear to ear at the thought of the good works they perform. You could be excused for thinking that you are on some kind of cyberspace Sunday School trip which is unconnected to the murky organization that Brown depicts. Opus Dei means "Work of God" in Latin and its motto is "Finding God in Work and Daily Life." It controls Vatican Radio and owns huge tracts of land and industry throughout the western world.

The full title of Opus Dei is "Prelature of the Holy Cross and Opus Dei." It was founded in Spain in 1928 and remains strong there. In fact, many aggressive religious orders, for example the Dominicans and the Jesuits, have their origins in Spain, perhaps partly as a result of its long struggle against Fascism and its historical role as a geographical bulwark against its spread.

Although officially a part of the Catholic Church, Opus Dei bears many of the hallmarks of a sect. Many top leaders of the Spanish military are said to be Opus Dei members. They no doubt feel at home in it. The organization is run with brutal efficiency; nobody is indispensable and orders are obeyed without question. Opus Dei in Spain has always targeted the most intelligent people from universities for recruitment. Because of the cloak-and-dagger atmosphere surrounding it, Opus Dei is often referred to there as the "Holy Mafia."

Despite controversy surrounding irregularities in the ecclesiastical processes and testimonials from thousands who had been harmed by Opus Dei, its founder, Msgr. Josemaría Escrivá de Balaguer, was ordained as a saint on October 6, 2002 after one of the shortest waiting times in history – he died in 1975. This suggests that the current Pope, John Paul II, is either a supporter of Opus Dei or is unaware of its true nature. Accounts of Josemaría Escrivá de Balaguer's life make clear that he was not even remotely pleasant to deal with. He was subject to fits of temper and was intolerant of anyone who was even faintly suspected of being anti-Opus Dei, including Pope John XXIII and Paul VI. The opinion was aired that his beatification could damage the whole ecclesiastical system.

Although some of the members are no doubt good natured and hold the best of intentions, it is indisputable that Opus Dei takes over the lives of its adherents in ways that its critics find most sinister.

There are an estimated 80,000 members worldwide, consisting of laity and priests. "Numerary" members of Opus Dei take an oath of celibacy and live in Opus Dei houses. They commit themselves to "the spirit of Opus Dei" without, perhaps, understanding the implications.

You do not have to be a Catholic or a male to join Opus Dei. Women are recruited from poor, rural and uneducated backgrounds as Numerary Assistants and also have to make a vow of celibacy. They are also responsible for the upkeep of the Opus Dei residences and are no doubt grateful for recent permission to wear trousers. Non-Catholics may join as Cooperators. This means that in exchange for perhaps a little Divine Grace in the manner of medieval indulgences, they pay large sums of money to Opus Dei.

Recruitment

The methods of recruiting are aggressive and underhanded. If a potential member is keen on a particular activity, Opus Dei members will organize a weekend centered on this activity to encourage him to join the "brethren." The Opus Dei-sponsored student group UNIV sometimes organizes trips to the Opus Dei headquarters in Rome during which the pressure for potential recruits to join is ratcheted up.

Members are encouraged to have a pool of twelve to fifteen friends, a number of which are likely candidates to "whistle" (join). They have to submit detailed statistical reports on the progress of the recruiting of these friends. Lonely, intelligent, attractive Catholics are the social profile most hunted down. Not only will they be best able to attract new members, but they are also likely to earn more for Opus Dei's coffers than other recruits. (Readers of The Da Vinci Code no doubt feel that recruiting would perhaps not be one of the Silas character's strong points.) Recruitment is also achieved through "front groups" at universities and other youth organizations. Often Opus Dei members do not reveal their identities as such. Pressure tactics are used to "close the deal." Potential recruits are encouraged to believe that they are at a crisis point in their lives and if they refuse to "whistle" they will lose God's grace.

The Life of a Member

Once they have joined, the Numerary Members are morally blackmailed into obeying all that they are told to do through the constant reminder of "the spirit of Opus Dei" to which they have agreed. From this point their lives are no longer their own. They are told about the idea of "childhood in front of God." Thus they hand over all decision-making to Opus Dei in the same way that children leave responsibility to their parents. This particularly appeals to the "eternal victim" type of personality, such as Silas in The Da Vinci Code.

Numeraries are usually college students or young professionals. They are housed in affluent city neighborhoods. These centers are staffed by a Director, an Assistant Director and a secretary.

This is the daily life that Numerary Members can expect:

– They take a vow of celibacy and practice "Corporal Mortification," which we will look at in a moment.

– In the manner of a playground bully asking a child for his lunch money, Opus Dei demands members to hand over their earnings. The members then have to request some of it to be returned to them for personal needs and they have to explain in detail how they spend their own money. They are usually not allowed to manage their own bank accounts. There is never any record of how Opus Dei spends the money it receives from its members in this way.

– Correspondence with the "outside world" is secretly monitored.

– All forms of entertainment are strictly controlled and censored, whether it be private or public entertainment. Members can watch television only in the company of a chaperone. Books must be pre-approved by the Director and usually only those written by the Founder, an Opus Dei member or a pre-Vatican II writer are permitted. In Article Number 339 of "The Way," the spiritual book of 999 articles mentioned in The Da Vinci Code, Josemaría Escrivá writes, "You shall not buy books without the advice of an experienced Christian. It is so easy to buy something useless or mischievous. Often people believe they are carrying a book under their arm...but they only carry a load of mud."

– All movements in and out of the Opus Dei residency are subject to permission from the member's Director.

– Members have to confess weekly, preferably only to an Opus Dei priest. They have to confess not only the normal run of misdemeanors, but any doubts that they may have on any aspect of Opus Dei. If not, in the charmingly poetic way that Opus Dei has of expressing such instances, "the mute devil takes over in the soul."

– Members' relationships with their families are discouraged on the grounds that they "will not understand." Members are supposed to destroy old family photographs. They are told what they can write in letters to relatives and what to say to them on the telephone. After telephone calls, they are interrogated on their content. Sometimes parents do not learn for months or even years that their children have become members. Similarly, friendships with those who are not marked for recruitment are difficult to maintain and the contact with their personal life in the outside world thus begins to become increasingly remote, eventually falling away entirely.

– All members must learn Spanish and Latin. Spanish is the language of the founder and Opus Dei prayers are recited in Latin.

Members are free to leave whenever they like, but the psychological tools that Opus Dei uses go into overdrive to ensure that this does not occur. Members are told that they will never lead a satisfying life if they leave and perhaps after all the indoctrination that has been inflicted upon them, that is correct. It is doubtful that Josemaría Escrivá himself could have borne a life of such restraint – the palace where he lived in Rome had 24 chapels alone. The present prelate of Opus Dei, Bishop Javier Echevarría (not to be confused with the fictional Manuel Aringarosa in *The Da Vinci Code*) was born in Madrid on June 14, 1932.

Corporal Mortification
Many of the painful practices involved in corporal mortification were common in the Catholic Church in the Middle Ages,

but, with the exception of fasting, they are now considered anachronistic. Ironically, it's considered that over-zealous attraction to pain can lead to pride and self-satisfaction.

The Opus Dei practices described in *The Da Vinci Code* are not exceptions. They form a routine part of the Numerary's daily life.

The Cilice

Brown cleverly uses the "cilice" to depict Silas as a typically indoctrinated Opus Dei member. A cilice is the spiked chain Silas wears around his upper thigh in *The Da Vinci Code*. It is obligatory to wear it for two hours a day, on Sundays, and at other prescribed times. Opus Dei is quite reluctant to talk about this. It leaves small prick holes in the skin, which makes Opus Dei members shy to undress in front of non-members. To prevent a member from getting masochistic pleasure out of this, he/she uses it under the spiritual supervision of a Director. Silas uses this instrument to dispel his "guilt" and it is one of the focuses of his obsession. It is perhaps difficult for us to believe in the twenty-first century western world that people in our midst are using the cilice in exactly the same way as Silas does, to willingly inflict physical damage upon themselves for religion's sake, but this is indeed what happens.

Discipline. A knotted cord is used as a whip on the buttocks or back once a week. Members have to ask permission to use it more than that. Many do.

Cold Showers. Many members take cold showers every day, which they offer up in honor of the prelate.

Meals. Numeraries usually abstain from at least one thing that they would consider to be a luxury at meal times. For example they may not take sugar in their tea, they eat unbuttered bread or toast or forgo a dessert. Members fast on certain days and apart from those obligations, have to ask permission to do so voluntarily. Again, many do.

The Heroic Minute. When they receive the wake up knock on their door in the morning, members are encouraged to jump out of bed, kiss the floor, and say "servium," which is Latin for "I will serve."

Silences. Members are not allowed to speak, even to say "Good night" or "Good morning" from the time that they make their confessions at night until after the Holy Mass of the next morning. In the afternoons, they generally do not speak until dinnertime. It is not a normal practice to listen to music on Sundays, especially in the afternoons.

There are gender differences in the corporal mortification that is used. For example, women sleep on boards which are laid on a mattress. Men sleep on the floor once a week. Both males and females sleep without a pillow once a week. Women are not allowed to smoke or enter bars. Men may smoke and are allowed to enter bars only for the purpose of recruiting new members. As a general rule, the founder, Josemaría Escrivá de Balaguer, considered women to have stronger passions than men and must be tamed accordingly.

In summation, for better or worse the true nature of Opus Dei is harsh and cruel, as revealed by its own literature. The following quotes are taken from the Opus Dei Awareness Network, Inc. website – www.odan.com:

"Blessed be pain. Loved be pain. Sanctified be pain... Glorified be pain!" (*The Way*, 208)

"No ideal becomes a reality without sacrifice. Deny yourself. It is so beautiful to be a victim!" (*The Way*, 175)

"Obey with your lips, your heart and your mind. It is not a man who is being obeyed, but God." (*Furrow*, maxim 374)

"And be watchful, for a spark is much easier to extinguish than a fire. Take flight, for in this it is low cowardice to be "brave"; a roving eye does not mean a lively spirit, but turns out to be a snare of Satan. Yet human diligence, with mortification, the cilice, disciplines and fasting are all worthless without you, my God." (Furrow, 834)

"They [Opus Dei numeraries] shall maintain the pious custom, for the purpose of chastising the body and reducing it to servitude, of wearing a small cilice for at least two hours daily; once a week they shall take the disciplines as well as sleeping on the floor, providing that health is not affected." (Opus Dei Constituciones, article 147)

"To defend his purity, St. Francis of Assisi rolled in the snow, St. Benedict threw himself into a thornbush, St. Bernard plunged into an icy pond... You... what have you done?" (The Way, 143)

"What has been lost through the flesh, the flesh should pay back: be generous in your penance." (The Forge, 207)

"If you realize that your body is your enemy, and an enemy of God's glory since it is an enemy of your sanctification, why do you treat it so softly?" (The Way, 227)

"Your worst enemy is yourself." (The Way, 225)

"You have come to the apostolate to submit, to annihilate yourself, not to impose your own personal viewpoints." (The Way, 936)

There is no doubt that Opus Dei performs a useful and charitable function in society, but it is tempting to conclude that it is better to be a beneficiary of the organization than a participant. Ultimately, it is not hard to see why Dan Brown chose members of Opus Dei to fill the role of villains in The DaVinci Code; in a sense the organization is an easy target, but perhaps that typecasting is justifiable.

Self Portrait of Leonardo da Vinci

Opposite page, top left: *The Madonna of the Rocks* by Leonardo da Vinci

Opposite page, top right:
The Mona Lisa by Leonardo da Vinci

Opposite page, bottom: *The Last Supper* by Leonardo da Vinci

This Page: *The Adoration of the Magi* by Leonardo da Vinci

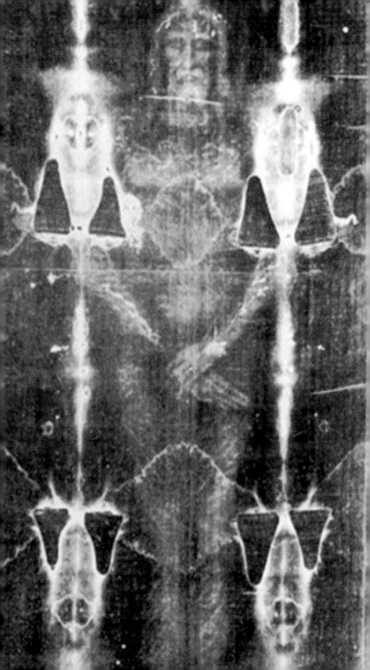

Left: The Shroud of Turin

Above: Woodcut of Grand Master of the Knights Templar, Jacques de Molay, his hands bound

Below: Knights Templar burned at the stake.

Top left: Nicolas Flamel's house in Paris, circa 1900 and, right, Flamel's house today

Above: Statue of Bérenger Saunière at the Saunière Museum (courtesy of Tracy Twyman)

Right: The Priory of Sion's official device

Opposite page, top: First Saunière parchment

Opposite page, bottom: Second Saunière parchment

ET FACTUM EST CUM IN
SABBATO SECUNDO PRIMO A
BI REPERSCCE TE DIS CIPULIA UTEM ILLIRISCOE
PERUNT UELLERE SPICAS ET FRICANTES MANIBUS + MANDU
CABANT QUIDAM AUTEM DE FARISAEIS AT
CEBANT EIE CCE QUIA FACIUNT DISCIPULI TUI SAB
BATIS + QUOD NON LICET RESPONDENS AUTEM INS
SET XTT ADE OS NUM QUAM HOC
LECISTIS QUOD FECIT DAUT DU... DO
ESURUTIP... ET QUICUM EOERAI + INTROIBIT IN DOMUM
DEI ET PANES PROPOSITIONIS   REDIS
MANDUCAUIT ET DEDIT ET QUI   BIES
CUM ERANTUXUO QUIBUS N O
NLICEDAT MANDUCARE SINON   SOLIS SACERDOTIBUS

JESUS CURGO ANTCCSEXATPES PASCSHAEVENJTTHETHQANTAMVKAT
SVEKAOTIAZA·VUSMORTYVVUS TVCMMJSVSCTYTAVITIYES VSFCACCKVRNT
LAVICM·TTCAENAPMTHTETOMARTHAHAMINISTRRABATTHASARVJO
VCROVNXVSCKATTC·DISCOVMENTATILVSCVJMMARTALENGOACHCEP
TILKTHRAMYNNGENTTJNARATPFTJTICITPRETTOVSTCTVNEXTTPC
DPCSTERVAETCXTEJRSTTICAYPIIRTJNJVISPCPCSCRTPTCTADOMBESTM
PLFTTAEJTEEXVUNGENTTTODAEREDIXALTERGOVRNVMCXAGTSCTPVAL
TJETVTXTVdAXJCAHJORTTJTVIYCKATCVHMTRADTTTVRVSTTVARCHOJCVN
HEN VIVMONONXVCNYTTGRECCENPATSDENAAKUSETAAATVMESGTE
GENTCS? DIXINVFCMHOCCNONTNTJTADCCGAENTJPERHATINELEAT
ADCVTMSEDTUNAFVRCLKTETLOVCVIOSHCAHENSECATNACMVTTIEHA
NMTVRPOTKAHETEATXTTCJRGOIESHVJSINEPTTILAMVNTTXdERCMS
CPVIGTVKAEMSCAESCRVNETILITTVdPAVPJERESENHTMSCMPGERHA
BEMTTSNOHLTISCVMFMEAUTETMNONSESMPERHAVHENSCJOGNO
VILTEROTZVKHAMVILTACXTMVDACTSTTVTATLOLTCESTXETVENE
AKVNTNONNPROTEPRTESUMETANTVMMJEdUTLUZAKUMPUTdCR
EH+TTVCMKSUSCTAOVITAMORRTVTSCPOGTTAVKERVNTAHVTCMP
RVTNCTPCJSSACEHCAOTVMVMTETLAZARVMTNATRFCTTRCNTT
LVTAMYLVTTPROPTCKILHXVMAHTHGNTCXVGTAZETSNETCRCA
DEHANTIINTESVM

JESU. MCACIA. VULNCRUM + SPCS. VNA. POXNITENTIVM.
PER. MAGDALANA. LACHYMAS + PCCCATA. NOSTRA. DILVAS.

Top left: Statue of Asmodeus
in the church at Rennes-le-Château
(courtesy of Tracy Twyman)

Top right: The Magdala Tower

Above: *Les Bergers d'Arcadie*
by Nicolas Poussin

Opposite page: The church at Rennes-
le-Château (courtesy of Tracy Twyman)

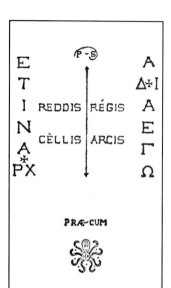

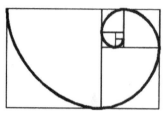

Top left: The Marie de Blanchefort tombstone from the graveyard at Rennes-le-Château, featuring the Priory's "PS" symbol

Top right: The Fibonacci Spiral

Bottom left: The Holy Grail Chalice in Valencia Cathedral

Bottom right: Pope John Paul II kissing the Chalice on November 8, 1982

Top: Medieval Fresco depicting the
Donation of Constantine in the Church
of Santi Quattro Coronati, Rome

Bottom left: Opus Dei headquarters
in New York

Bottom right: Baphomet drawn
by French occultist Eliphas Lévi

Le Pendu.

The Tarot card of the Hanging Man,
attributed to Jacquemin Gringonneur

Top: The Louvre

Bottom: La Pyramide Inversée
at the Louvre

Top left: L'Église de Saint-Sulpice

Top right: The "Rose Line"
(supposedly the original, ancient)
Meridian running through l'Église de
Saint-Sulpice

Bottom: Le Château de Villette

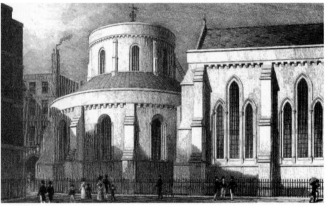

Top: Rosslyn Chapel

Bottom: The Temple Church in London, as restored. Drawn by Tho. H. Shepherd, engraved by J. Carter. published Aug. 16, 1828, Jones & Co, London

Left: The Apprentice pillar, Rosslyn Chapel (courtesy of Lisa Fong)

Westminster Abbey in London
(courtesy of LaLa (Imre Olajos, Jr))

Chapter Ten
Other Themes Explored in
The Da Vinci Code

Cryptology and the Atbash Cipher

The term cryptology comes from the Greek *kryptós*, "hidden," and *lógos*, "word."

The first recorded use of cryptology for correspondence was by the Greek Spartans in about 400 BC. They used what is called a skytale so that military commanders could communicate secretly. A message was written on a piece of leather or parchment and wrapped spirally around a tapered baton. When unwrapped, the message appeared to be a jumble of letters, and could only be read when put around another tapered baton of exactly the same size and proportions.

The Atbash cipher is a system in which the last letter represents the first, and the second letter the second to last.

In the Roman alphabet, it appears like this:

PLAINTEXT   a b c d e f g h i j k l m
CIPHERTEXT Z Y X W V U T S R Q P O N
PLAINTEXT   n o p q r s t u v w x y z
CIPHERTEXT M L K J I H G F E D C B A

The cipher was discovered by Dr. Hugh J. Schonfield. Dr. Schonfield was one of the original researchers working on the Dead Sea Scrolls at Qumran and his most notable book on Biblical history is *The Passover Plot*. He applied the code to some of the scrolls that were otherwise indecipherable to his fellow researchers. It had been used to conceal names in Essene/Zadokite/Nazarean texts in the first century. In fact, it was used as early as 500 BC by scribes writing the Book of Jeremiah. It is one of the few code systems that are used in the Hebrew language.

In *The Messianic Legacy*, Baigent, Leigh and Lincoln write that Dr. Schonfield describes in *The Essene Odyssey* how he became fascinated by the Baphomet that was worshiped by the Knights Templar and applied the Atbash cipher to the word "Baphomet." To his surprise, he found that the word decoded itself into *Sophia*, the Greek word for "wisdom."

The word "Baphomet" in Hebrew is as follows, bearing in mind that Hebrew is read right to left:

[taf] [mem] [vav] [pe] [bet]

Applying the Atbash cipher to the above, Schonfield found the following:

[alef] [yud] [pe] [vav] [shin]

which results in *Sophia*, the Greek word written in Hebrew right to left.

Sophia doesn't only mean "wisdom." *Sophia* was also the goddess who was supposed to be the bride of God. Many believe that the Knights Templar worshiped this goddess.

The fact that the Knights Templar were familiar with the Atbash cipher strongly suggests that there were people around from a Nazarean sect at the time of the Knights Templar who were familiar with the code.

Dan Brown's idea that English is the "purest" language may be fanciful, but it is not new. Abbé Henri Boudet of Rennes-le-Bains, a neighboring village of Renne-le-Château, wrote a book called *Le Vrai Langue Celtique*, claiming that English was a sacred language which had perhaps been spoken before the time of the destruction of the Tower of Babel. It has been said that the book is not meant to be taken literally and conveyed a different message, written in code. We also have to bear in mind that, similar to many other European languages, many English words have their roots in Latin. As Tracy Twyman in the pages of her *Dagobert's Revenge* magazine points out, the English language has 26 letters and so can be used perfectly with the Atbash Code. Other European languages do not have an even number of letters. Additionally, she has always thought that the Priory of Sion favored the English language.

The Cryptex

This appears to be an instance of *The Da Vinci Code*'s author exercising his poetic license and creating a completely fictional device. I could find no evidence that "The Cryptex" ever existed in real life, although it is perhaps not entirely unlikely that Leonardo could have come up with such an invention.

Baphomet

Brewer's Dictionary of Phrase and Fable tells us that "Baphomet" is a corruption of "Mahomet" or "Mohammed" in English, the Muslim prophet. As the Templars associated themselves with the Muslim Hashashin, some believe that they adopted Muslim ways, but this ignores the fact that the Muslim religion forbids idolatry. There is also the theory that the word comes from the joining of two Greek words meaning "absorption into wisdom." During their persecution, the Knights Templar were accused of worshipping an idol named Baphomet. It was said to take the form of either a head or a black cat.

It is believed that the imagery of the Baphomet derives from the ancient Egyptian god Amon, meaning "The Hidden One" who is also known as the Goat of Mendes.

To a great extent, the beliefs about Baphomet have been subject to the fashion of the age. In the nineteenth century it was popular to consider the Knights Templar as devil worshipers, whereas in the twentieth and twenty-first centuries the belief that they were battling against a corrupt government and church is more prevalent. However, the story about Baphomet has survived.

The Dictionary of the Occult and Supernatural by Peter Underwood gives us the following definition:

> Baphomet was the deity worshipped by the Knights Templar, and in Black Magic as the source and creator of evil; the Satanic goat of the witches' Sabbath and one of the names adopted by Aleister Crowley.

Eliphas Lévi (real name Alphonse Louis Constant) the nineteenth century occultist, described some of the more common and varied descriptions of Baphomet:

– An idol with a human skull

– A head with two faces

– With a beard

– Without a beard

– With the head of a cockerel

– With the head of a man

– With the head of a goat and the body of a man but with wings and cloven feet (the Sabbatic Goat)

The last concept of the Sabbatic Goat that he depicts led to the present-day perception of the devil. As Dan Brown tells us in *The Da Vinci Code*, Baphomet's head became that of the Christian devil. The sign of the devil, the two fingers raised behind a friend's head, that he also mentions as being jokingly employed in group photographs, is also used in southern Europe to signify a cuckold. Both British occultist Aleister Crowley and Church of Satan founder Anton LaVey later adopted the Baphomet imagery. It was only under the torture that was meted out to the Templars at the hands of the French King, Philippe, who was in collusion with Pope Clement V, that the Templars admitted to the worship of a large idol of the demon. The Grand Master of the Templars, Jacques de Molay, as he was roasting to death on the spit, said that the only thing that the Templars were guilty of was lying under torture.

According to Tracy Twyman, co-author of *Vessel of God*, when the Templars' Paris preceptory was raided another Baphomet head was found. This was described as "a great head of gilded silver, most beautiful, and consisting of an image of a woman. Inside were two head bones wrapped in a cloth of white linen, with another red cloth around it. There was a label attached upon which was written the legend 'Caput 58M.'"

Other depictions of the origin of the Baphomet include the head of John the Baptist, who was considered by the Templars to be the true messiah, in favor of Christ who was considered to be false. The image that Eliphas Lévi propagated of the Baphomet now illustrates the Devil in the Waite version of the Tarot cards as half male, half female, half human, half animal. As the Baphomet is depicted with not only women's breasts but men's sexual organs, he is androgyne. The purpose of this image was to indicate the struggle between two conflicting opposites. Some readers may recall that Marilyn Manson also utilized Lévi's Baphomet at one point in his "branding."

The Fibonacci Sequence and the Golden Ratio

The "Fibonacci Sequence" was the invention of the mathematician Leonardo Fibonacci (born in about 1170, probably in Pisa, died after 1240.) He was also known as Leonardo Pisano. In 1202 he wrote *Liber Abaci* ("Book of the Abacus"). He was the first European to work on Indian and Arabian mathematics. His father was appointed consul for a community of Pisan merchants in what is now Algeria and Leonardo studied mathematics under an Arabic tutor. He also studied mathematics in Egypt, Syria, Greece, Sicily and Provence.

When *Liber Abaci* first appeared, the Hindu-Arabic numerals were known only to a few intellectuals. The book soon spread very quickly and drew the attention of Holy Roman emperor Frederick II. Leonardo was invited to appear before him where he was asked to solve various mathematical problems. This was the start of several years' correspondence with Frederick II and his scholars, exchanging mathematical problems.

The Fibonacci Sequence derived from a problem in *Liber Abaci*:

> *A certain man put a pair of rabbits in a place surrounded on all sides by a wall. How many pairs of rabbits can be produced from that pair in a year if it is supposed that every month each pair begets a new pair which from the second month on becomes productive?*

The resulting sequence is, as Dan Brown tells us, 1-1-2-3-5-8-13-21, and then goes on to 34-55 and on forever. Each number is the sum of the two preceding numbers and it was the first such number sequence known in Europe.

The mathematician Robert Simson at the University of Glasgow discovered in 1753 that as the numbers got greater, the ratio between succeeding numbers approached the number Φ, the golden ratio, or the Divine Proportion or its Greek name "Phi." It is the number 1.6180339887498948482 which is similar to "Pi" in that its decimal points go on into infinity without repeating the sequence. It can be calculated exactly using this formula: $\Phi = (1 + \sqrt{5}) / 2$.

In a Golden Rectangle, the ratio of the length to the width is the Golden Ratio. Therefore if one side of the rectangle is 3 units, the other side will be 3 x 1.62 = 4.86.

The term Fibonacci Sequence was first used by the French mathematician Edouard Lucas. From this point onwards scientists began to note more and more examples of such sequences in nature, for example, the spirals of a sunflower head, in pine cones, the arrangement of leaf buds on a stem, the growth pattern of seeds into plants and animal horns. Also the growth pattern of human beings goes through the stages of fetus, baby, child, adult using the Golden Ratio.

Take any Golden Rectangle using the above formula and you will find that if you remove a square from it, you will be left with another smaller Golden Rectangle. Constant removal of squares from the resulting Golden Rectangles will result in smaller and smaller Golden Rectangles.

Similarly with the Fibonacci Sequence, you can do the opposite by starting with a square of measurement unit 1. Add a square of the same size and you will form a rectangle. If you continue adding squares to the longer sides of the rectangles that you form, the longer sides will be successive Fibonacci numbers, and you will eventually reach a Golden Rectangle.

Draw two squares measuring 1 x 1 each, next to each other, and then draw a 2 x 2 square next to them. Then draw a square measuring 3 x 3 on the edge of one 1 x 1 side combined with one 2 x 2 side. The next step is to put a 5 x 5 next to the 3 x 3 and 2 x 2, and the spiral effect will become apparent. If, as is inevitable, the piece of paper you are using runs out, draw in the spiral itself, connecting one corner of each square to the opposite corner with a curve. The Parthenon in Athens fits into a Golden Rectangle. Leonardo da Vinci and more modern artists such as Seurat and Mondrian also used this geometry.

The solar system itself is a Fibonacci spiral, acting as a vortex, of which the center is the Sun. In fact Leonardo said, "A vortex, unlike a wheel, moves faster to its center." For example Mercury's year lasts 88 Earth days whereas Pluto's lasts 248 Earth years. According to Tracy Twyman and Boyd Rice in *Vessel of God*, it goes even further than that: the distance between the Sun and Mercury added to that between Mercury and Venus equals that between Venus and Earth.

Secret Societies

The Da Vinci Code's main theme is the effect that at least one secret society, the Priory of Sion, has had on history and all our lives as a consequence. Secret societies have been around since the dawn of human existence because men have always felt the need to manipulate world events behind the scenes, whether for good or evil. A secret society is often referred to as a "cabal." This word originated with a committee of five ministers under Charles II of England whose surnames began with C, A, B, A and L. In some religious traditions, such as Judaism and Buddhism, there exist cabals of carefully chosen individuals, living throughout the world, who ensure that the world operates in the way that their God intends. In Buddhism this involves the reincarnation from one generation to the next of "Secret Masters."

There are, of course, degrees of secrecy and to a greater or lesser extent secrets exist in all religions. The inner order of the Jesuit arm of the Catholic Church was until recently the Holy Office, otherwise known as the Inquisition. That has now developed into Opus Dei, discussed in Chapter Nine. The Rosicrucians managed to maintain such a high degree of secrecy that some suspect the Order may not have even existed at all. And of course, the Priory of Sion is about as secretive as is possible.

The most familiar "secret" society today is Freemasonry, which is no doubt the largest secret society in the Western world. It has the ambiguous identity of being both a positive charitable organization, and, some suspect, something more sinister – at least in its upper echelons.

Other present day societies that can be considered "secret" include the Mafia, the Trilateral Commission, the Bilderberg Group, the Skull & Bones Society, Bohemian Grove, and according to some, the Illuminati (prominently featured in Dan Brown's first Robert Langdon novel, *Angels & Demons*). As well as being powerful in their own right, they also have the ability to inspire fear and it is in this way that they exercise their greatest controlling power.

Throughout history, such people as Charles Nodier, who was reputed to be one of the Grand Masters of the Priory of Sion, played upon the fear that secret societies inspire. He would invent societies, write about them and then accuse perfectly innocent people of belonging to them. This provoked the hapless individuals involved to form themselves into a real secret society to offer each other mutual protection, rendering the fictitious secret society an omen of the real one, a self-fulfilling prophecy.

One's perspective of any secret society is likely to be at least partly formed by whether or not one is a member of it. The secret society that Dan Brown deals with in *The Da Vinci Code* is the Priory of Sion which, we are led to believe through the evidence, has operated powerfully and under wraps for centuries. There have also been several secret societies that are suspected of an association with the Priory of Sion.

The Sovereign and Military Order of the Temple of Jerusalem

This society was founded in its present form in only 1804. However, they claim that Jacques de Molay, the last Grand Master of the Knights Templar, left a charter legitimizing their society when he was executed in 1314. This charter is generally thought to be genuine, although some historians doubt its authenticity. As the order is largely devoted to charitable works, it is not perceived as a threat.

Baigent, Leigh and Lincoln met its Grand Master several times in 1982. They were told that a faction had broken away and established itself as a neo-Templar organization in Switzerland and that it was run by Anton Zapelli. This name rang a bell with Baigent, Leigh and Lincoln as they had been told some years before that a person named Zapelli was the real power behind the Priory of Sion. After some investigation they discovered that Zapelli was involved not only in private banking, but in the establishment of "the role of modern Templars in the reunification of Europe," which, according to Zapelli, was the original intention of the Templars. What they meant by "Europe" was the countries stretching from the Atlantic and the Mediterranean to the Urals of western Russia. They have almost achieved what they claimed to want in the present European Union, which currently spreads from Ireland in the west to Poland in the east.

P2

P2 (its full name is Raggruppamento Gelli Propaganda Due), founded in 1966, is a Masonic Lodge which was also involved in the fight against communism. In the opinion of the leader of Italy's Republican Party at the time, P2 became "the center of pollution of national life – secret, perverse, and corrupting." It brought down the government of premier Arnaldo Forlani. It acted as a conduit for the supply of funds from the Vatican and the CIA to anti-communist organizations in Europe and Latin America. P2 was exposed when "God's banker," Roberto Calvi, was found murdered, hanging under London's Blackfriars Bridge in 1982. Calvi funneled millions of Vatican dollars to the Polish revolutionary group "Solidarity." When Calvi's own private bank was in trouble, he went to the Vatican for help, making vague threats that he would expose the origin of Solidarity's support. He lived for a further twelve days before his untimely death – and the disappearance of his briefcase, which the Vatican later bought for about 10 million euros.

Some say that P2 was (and probably still is) controlled by the Mafia. Others that the KGB, CIA or even the Priory of Sion are responsible.

The way in which P2 operated was through the Grand Master, Licio Gelli, convincing potential members that he had huge influence and they believed that Gelli could pave the way for their own personal greater success. This system was self-perpetuating and Gelli's power increased exponentially. He managed to extract official secrets from his members that he could use both to increase his power and to blackmail others.

In 1981, after the police raided Gelli's premises, they found the membership lists, which were published in the Italian press. One of the headings was "Opus Dei" and one of the members was listed as Giulio Andreotti, the Christian Democratic politician who was six times Prime Minister of Italy and alleged to be a member of the Priory of Sion. In 1995 he was accused of selling political favors to the Mafia and of complicity in the murder of a journalist in 1979. In 1999 he was acquitted of both charges. This decision was upheld in the appeals court in 2003.

The Sovereign and Military Order of the Temple of Jerusalem was also mentioned in the P2 membership list.

Compagnie de Saint-Sacrement

The Compagnie de Saint-Sacrement was founded between 1627 and 1629. Some consider it to be so similar to the Priory of Sion that they were in fact the same organization or that the Priory controlled the Compagnie. It is a rare example of a secret society whose history is well documented. The Priory of Sion documents claim that the Priory "dedicated itself to deposing Mazarin," and refer often to the Compagnie. It was Mazarin, in the seventeenth century, who acted as chief minister of France under Louis XIV. His administration was so unpopular that opposition to him initiated the civil wars that are referred to as "the Fronde."

The Compagnie is well-known in France. However it was so secretive that even its members were unaware of who ran it and initiates were led to believe that it was devoted to charitable work. Its influence radiated from the Seminary of Saint-Sulpice in Paris, which is where the character of Silas tries to find the "keystone" in *The Da Vinci Code*. In fact Jean-Jacques Olier, the founder of Saint-Sulpice, was closely associated with the Compagnie. Other well-known families who were connected with the Fronde and the Priory of Sion were also associated with it. At the center of the activities of the Compagnie was what is referred to as "the Secret," the identity of which nobody is aware. It is now thought that its activities involved espionage, particularly in royal circles and other institutions such as the legal profession, the police, and the government. Although its *raison d'être* was supposedly to oppose heresy, it was accused of heresy itself by Catholic authorities.

King Louis XIV ordered the Compagnie to disband in 1660, but his wishes were successfully ignored for five years until

1665. All its documents were collected and deposited in an unknown place, suspected to be Saint-Sulpice. The Compagnie seemed merely to go underground, however, and it was said to survive into the twentieth century. In 1667, the French playwright and staunch royalist, Molière, staged a play called *Le Tartuffe* which had clear and damaging references to the Compagnie. The Compagnie showed its continuing influence by getting the play banned for two years.

The Origins of Tarot

The origins of the "Game of Tarot" are obscure, but it was likely to have been introduced into France to amuse the jaded and manically depressed Charles VI who reigned from 1380 to 1422. It also appeared in Italy at about the same time. The tarot was used in France as an amusement until relatively recently. Some cards, dating from the fourteenth and fifteenth centuries, which show figures similar to those found on present day tarot cards, have survived. A simple card game which included theological "Virtues and Vices" was played in Italy. The author of the tarot as we now know it was likely to be one of the Hebrew cabbalists who wanted to present ancient Eastern wisdom into Europe and modernized the symbols accordingly. He was no doubt aware of the power of using the medium of a pastime to get his message across effectively. A similar recent example is the pack of cards published by the American military with the images of wanted Iraqis. Dan Brown's assertion in *The Da Vinci Code* that the tarot describes the story of "the Lost Bride and her subjugation by the evil church" is perhaps far-fetched but not impossible.

Contrary to what Brown says, as Tracy Twyman and Boyd Rice state in their book *Vessel of God*, it is a proven, though little known fact that the Minor Arcana derives from the modern card pack and not the other way around.

There is no evidence that it was used for fortune telling until the end of the sixteenth or beginning of the seventeenth centuries. Significantly, neither Paracelsus nor

Boissard mention the tarot in their treatises on divination in the sixteenth century. The first mention of the tarot's use in this way was in a book published in Frankfurt in the early seventeenth century. It was not used widely for divination until the eighteenth century and was first employed by Gypsies. From the eighteenth century, tarot's association with the esoteric was established by different writers and we have inherited these ideas.

However, the symbolism of some of the cards in the Major Arcana dates back to at least the second century AD. Egyptian culture had had a strong influence on Greek culture and the concept of divine unity, of which the Sun was an important component, endured. The knowledge behind their beliefs was conveyed in symbols of which only initiates knew the key. The external rituals of their religion served simply as a physical manifestation of these beliefs.

Such symbols may be associated with the tarot in which the Major Arcana (22 cards) can be interpreted as spiritual matters and trends in the questioner's life, while the Minor Arcana (56 cards) reflects business and career matters. The use of such symbolism is seen in Chinese characters and even western heraldry.

The tarot could therefore be said to be a book written in symbols that emanate from the ideas of ancient Egypt, Asia Minor and the Science of the Universe as it was perceived in the second century. However, as Twyman and Rice point out, many scholars also speculate that playing cards were brought and adapted to Europe by the Knights Templar and that the descendants of Templars had a decisive role in the formation of the tarot.

Dan Brown writes that swords correspond to spades in present-day playing cards, hearts to cups, clubs to scepters (or wands) and diamonds to pentacles. However it is generally accepted that clubs correspond to pentacles and diamonds to wands. The modern tarot pack is based upon the Venetian or Piedmontese tarot. Each card has its own meaning: wands are associated with business matters, cups with love, swords with conflict and pentacles with money and material comfort. The cards are laid out in front of the questioner by the fortune-teller and a few cards are selected by either the fortune-teller or the questioner in what is known as a "spread." The meaning of the card is dependent on whether or not it is upside down, its position in the spread and the cards that precede and follow it.

History of the Vatican Observatory and Castel Gandalfo

The Vatican Observatory

The Vatican Observatory is reputed to be one of the oldest astronomical institutions in the world. It can first be traced to Pope Gregory XIII setting up a committee to look into the scientific implications of reforming the calendar in 1582. Since that time the Papacy has expressed interest in astronomical matters and founded three early observatories – the Observatory of the Roman College (1774 – 1878), the Observatory of the Capitol (1827 – 1870), and the Specula Vaticana (1789 – 1821) in the Tower of the Winds which is situated inside the Vatican. In the nineteenth century, the well-known Jesuit Father Angelo Secchi broke new ground by classifying the stars according to their spectra. In answer to an accusation of the Catholic Church ignoring the advance of science, the Specula Vaticana was re-founded in 1891 by Pope Leo XIII and located on a hillside behind the dome at St. Peter's Basilica. The intention was to map out the whole sky, but it was moved to Castel Gandolfo in 1936 (see below.) Participants in the Observatory's activities were made by the various religious orders, including the Augustinians and Jesuits. One of the most notable was Johann Georg Hagen, a Jesuit priest and astronomer who discovered and studied dark clouds of tenuous, interstellar matter sometimes known as Hagen's clouds. In 1906 Pope Pius X appointed him director of the Vatican Observatory. In 1981, because of the continuing encroachment of light affecting observations, the Observatory was moved again, this time as the Vatican Observatory Research Group (VORG) in Tucson, Arizona. The Vatican Advanced Technology Telescope is now situated at Mount Graham, Arizona.

Castel Gandolfo

The village and castle of Castel Gandolfo is situated in the Roma *provincia* in the Lazio (Latium) *regionel*, in central Italy. It is on the shores of Lake Albano, about 35 kilometers southeast of Rome, and has been a summer residence of the Popes since the construction of the Apolostolic, or Papal, Palace.

Its name originates from the castle which belonged to the ducal Gandalfi family of the twelfth century. Construction of the Palace was begun by Pope Urban VIII who reigned as Pope from 1623 – 1644. It is officially part of the Vatican State and the former Villa Barberini was built on the ruins of a villa of the Roman Emperor Domitian. It housed the Vatican Observatory from 1936 when it was realized that the lights of Rome were preventing the furthest stars from being observed at the Observatory in Vatican City. Two new telescopes and an astrophysical laboratory were installed. The Castle library has about 22,000 books including rare antique books by Copernicus, Galileo and Sir Isaac Newton. The village was used in the 1960 Olympic Games for the rowing events and the area has a reputation for peaches, wine and fish from the lake.

The Gnostic Gospels

The word Gnostic comes from the Greek *gnosis* meaning "knowledge," especially esoteric knowledge. Gnosticism is a system of religious dualism; that is the belief that the co-equal powers of good and evil ruled the universe.[7] Some also believed in "Abraxas," who was believed to be omnipotent and both good and evil.

---

[7] Some Gnostics believed that the material world, ruled by the God who created it, "Rex Mundi" (King of the World) is evil, whereas the spiritual world, which was created by the God who rules it, was considered to be good.

The term "Abraxas" was used by the Basilideans who were a second century Gnostic sect. The magical word "Abracadabra" derives from this name. Their belief was that Jesus Christ had come from Abraxas and lived as a phantom on Earth. They attached special significance to the name Abraxas as it contains all seven of the Greek letters that add up to 365, the number of days in three out of four years. As an extension of this, Abraxas was believed to rule over 365 gods who each possessed a virtue, meaning that each day of the year was assigned a specific virtue.

The Gnostic Gospels ultimately feel under the category of what is referred to as the New Testament Apocrypha. The term "Apocrypha" originally meant that the writings were secret and they were accepted only by some Christians and minority heretical groups. From the fourth century onwards it came to refer to books that were not read publicly in church. Eventually their status in the eyes of the church diminished to the extent that they were said to be forgeries.

The Gnostic Gospels are written in the names of, or about, the apostles, but were not by them. They were written during the second century AD, before the list of accepted books of New Testament was drawn up. Originally there were many different gospels, but in 367 AD, Bishop Athanasius of Alexandria selected some of the writings and these texts were then agreed and approved at the Council of Hippo in 393 AD. The list was cut down further later on and finally it was only the Gospels of Matthew, Mark, Luke and John which were approved.

These writings were gradually excluded from Christian reading, both public and private. Most have survived only as fragments but some have been found in Greek and Coptic papyrus from Egypt. They reflect popular beliefs of the day about Christ, his followers and Christian traditions. The clergy believed that what was written about Christ in these books was false and so did not give their permission for them to be read.

The Gospel of Philip, which *The Da Vinci Code's* Leigh Teabing says "is always a good place to start," is one of the Gospels ascribed to the Twelve Apostles and is what is known as a Valentinian Gnostic treatise. Valentinus was an Egyptian religious philosopher who founded the Roman and Alexandrian schools of Gnosticism. The Gospel of Philip is a collection of about one hundred short excerpts from sources of Christian Gnostic instruction. It details initiation rites and the meanings of names, especially that of Jesus. More controversially, and probably one of the reasons why Teabing finds it so appealing, is that it states, "Some say Mary was conceived by the Holy Spirit. They are wrong. They do not know what they are saying." The gospel was found in the Codices of the Nag Hammadi papyri, a collection of thirteen codices of Gnostic scriptures and commentaries written in the second or third century (although the codices themselves are fourth-century copies) which were found in 1945. Nag Hammadi is situated on the west bank of the Nile, in Upper Egypt, on or near the site of the ancient town of Chenoboskion.

Chapter Eleven
Significant Parisian Locations
Visited in *The Da Vinci Code*

The Louvre

La Musée du Louvre is the national museum and art gallery of France. It is situated in part of a large palace that was built on the site of the twelfth century fortress of Philip Augustus. King Francis I had it demolished and the present building was constructed. He was a great art collector and subsequent monarchs added both to the Louvre and the art collection during their reigns.

When Louis XIV moved his court to Versailles, the Louvre ceased to be a royal palace and it was first used as a public gallery in the eighteenth century. In the 1980s and 1990s the museum was refurbished in order to ease access to the public. A large complex of amenities and a shopping mall was opened under the Louvre and the controversial steel-and-glass pyramid was built in the courtyard (the Cour Napoleon) which had been designed by the American architect, I.M. Pei. He also designed the new wing which has an area of 230,000 square feet.

The pyramid does not have 666 panes of glass, as Dan Brown claims, but 675 diamond shaped and 118 rectangular panes. It is 79 feet tall and flanked by three smaller pyramids.

The Louvre's collection of fifteenth – nineteenth century paintings is without parallel in the world and the rest of the gallery covers a vast area of art, antiquities and many treasures that belonged to the French royal family.

La Pyramide Inversée is located in the underground shopping mall just west of the Louvre to which it connects. The whole structure is made of glass which allows sunlight to enter.

L'Église de Saint-Sulpice

The Church of Saint-Sulpice is situated on the corner of rue Paletine on Place de Sulpice. It has two towers and the church has a heavy and massive look to it. On the left-hand tower there is, perhaps incongruously, the Hebrew inscription JAHWE. The plan of the church and the size are the same as of Nôtre Dame. The construction of the church started in 1646 on the remains of a smaller church. As there were interruptions to the building, there are many different architectural styles represented. The copper line representing the Paris meridian line, or "roseline," runs through the choir. The precursor of the telegraph, known as the Chappe system, which was a visual signal line between Paris and Rouen, was fixed on the roof and used until 1850. Baudelaire and the Marquis de Sade were baptized in the church and Victor Hugo got married there in a special ceremony in 1822.

Jean-Jacques Olier founded the Seminary of Saint-Sulpice (the Sulpicians) and was associated with the Compagnie de Saint-Sacrement, which we looked at in detail in Chapter Ten's section on Secret Societies. The church is thought to have been the center of its activities. When the documents of the Compagnie de Saint-Sacrement were recalled because of continued opposition from Louis XIV, they are thought to have been hidden in Saint-Sulpice.

The Sulpicians dedicated themselves to the training of candidates for the priesthood and the order was named after Sulpicius, a bishop of Bourges in Merovingian times. They founded the city of Montreal in Canada, and built Nôtre-Dame Basila there in 1829. Interestingly their symbol is two M's, one upside down upon the other.

The Catholic Modernist movement was an organization that was founded in order to train experts to defend the literal meaning of the Bible. The idea backfired, however, as the more the "experts" studied the subject and noted the various inconsistencies in the Bible, the less they felt convinced of the truth of what was written. The Church eventually accused them of being Freemasons. The headquarters of the Modernist Movement was Saint-Sulpice.

Rue Haxo

This street starts at rue du Surmelin, 39 and finishes at boulevard Sérurier, 67. It stretches from the nineteenth to the 20th arrondissements (districts) of Paris. There are no buildings between numbers 16 and 36; *The Da Vinci Code's* Depository Bank of Zurich was supposedly at number 24, which does not exist. Neither does the bank, although the book's publisher, Doubleday/Random House, has created a fake website at www.depositorybankofzurich.com

Le Château de Villette

The castle where *The Da Vinci Code's* Leigh Teabing lives is situated 35 minutes northwest of Paris near Versailles. It was designed by architect Francois Mansart in about 1668 for Jean Dyel, the Comte d'Aufflay, Louis XIV's ambassador to Venice and was finished in about 1696 by his nephew Jules Hardouin-Mansart. It is one of the most important châteaux in France and is now available for meetings, seminars, vacations, weddings and other special events. It has eleven bedrooms. There are two rectangular-shaped lakes in the 185 acre grounds. The Palace of Versailles was designed at the same time as le Château de Villette.

Chapter Twelve
Rosslyn Chapel

As Dan Brown points out in *The Da Vinci Code*, Rosslyn Chapel is nicknamed the "Cathedral of Codes." It is also known as "the Tapestry in Stone" and in some cases, "a garden in stone." All these epithets are more descriptively beguiling than its "Christian" name of St. Matthew's Collegiate Church, which it uses in its capacity as a fully operational Episcopalian chapel. They indicate, quite rightly, that Rosslyn Chapel has a message which goes far beyond that of other Christian buildings. In fact, Professor Philip Davis, the eminent biblical and Dead Sea Scrolls scholar, says that there is nothing at all Christian about the building apart from its nineteenth century additions. He concluded that the reason it was built was to conceal a medieval secret. Because of its association with the founding of Freemasonry it was also known as "Lodge Number One" in Edinburgh. It is located in the village of Rosslyn (or "Roslin") near Edinburgh above the Esk Valley, a few miles from the original Templar center at "Ballantradoch," meaning "the House of the Warrior."

In *The Da Vinci Code*, Robert Langdon tells Sophie Neveu that the word "Roslin" means "Line of the Rose," but other explanations exist. Some say that "Roslin" is a Gaelic word meaning "ancient knowledge passed down the generations" while others break the word down into the Celtic "ros" ("a promontary") and "lin" ("waterfall"). Yet another, perhaps more interesting translation is "stone falling from heaven," a phrase with Masonic, alchemical and Luciferian implications. Perhaps the least attractive definition comes from *Cassell's Dictionary of Scottish Names*, which translates the word to mean "morass at a pool."

Rosslyn Chapel was built for the Prince of Orkney, Sir William Saint Clair, and it was apparently completed by his son Oliver in 1486. The name "Saint Clair" (now "Sinclair") comes from the Latin "Sanctus Claris" meaning "Holy Light." The stone from which it was built has been identified by Dr. Jack Miller, the Head of Studies of Geology at Cambridge University, as coming from exactly the same strata as that found in Jerusalem. As Dan Brown indicates in *The Da Vinci Code* and as authors Christopher Knight and Robert Lomas prove in their book *The Hiram Key*, the floor plan of Rosslyn is nearly identical to that of the Temple of Solomon. The oversized western wall is particularly reminiscent of the ruins of Herod's Temple. The pillars of Boaz and Jachin, which stood at the entrance to Solomon's Temple, are in exactly the same position at Rosslyn Chapel. Furthermore, the huge engrailed cross of Saint Clair on the ceiling points to exactly the spot in the floor plan where the "Holy of Holies" was kept at the Temple of Solomon.

When the Knights Templar built cathedrals throughout Europe in the medieval period, they accepted their stonemasons into the lower grades of the Templar order. Following the demise of the Templars' power, these stonemasons continued the observance and practice of these rituals on mainland Europe. Sir William Saint Clair decided to hire these ex-Templar stonemasons from Europe, instead of local Scottish stonemasons, to build Rosslyn Chapel. It was in this manner that Scottish Rite Freemasonry was born and the Saint Clairs became its hereditary patrons and Grand Masters, which they are to this very day.

The Saint Clairs came from Normandy and had been one of the most influential familes in Europe since the tenth century. At first they seemed to threaten the line of King David I of Scotland, who reigned from 1124 to 1153. The Saint Clairs had been invested with the Barony of Roslin in 1057 by the Scots King Malcolm III, also known as Malcolm Canmore ("the Bigheaded"). Marie de Saint Clair was married to the first Grand Master of the Priory of Sion, Jean de Gisors. The Priory of Sion, as we know, was formed from the related Order of the Temple. And of course, one of the most recent Grand Masters of the Priory is Pierre Plantard de Saint-Clair, who claims descent from this family. In *The Da Vinci Code*, Robert and Sophie are led by a series of clues to Rosslyn, where they discover Sophie's long-lost mother and brother, whom, up until that point, she has been led to believe were dead. She discovers that they are members of the Saint Clair family, the hereditary protectors of the chapel.

The interior walls and ceilings of Rosslyn Chapel are festooned with symbols of Freemasonry, Templarism, Judaism and Christianity, along with a few Islamic motifs. Although the abundance of carvings appears to be a discordant cacophony, each element is there for a reason and relates strongly to its neighbors. Readers of *The Da Vinci Code* will recall how mesmerized Robert Langdon was by the plethora of symbolism he found at Rosslyn Chapel. It is here that Robert and Sophie discover a code pointing towards the six-pointed Seal of Solomon – emblematic, writes Dan Brown, of the chalice and the blade, the union of male and female energies embodied in the Grail symbol.

A monument to the Pagan "Green Man" or "Jack of the Green" welcomes you when you enter. You notice that his vacant, eerie, and hollow eyes have an unnerving way of following your progress around the chapel. It is said that this monument is consistently colder than the stones that surround it and some say that it is difficult, if not impossible, to photograph.

The Apprentice Pillar is a dominant feature of the Chapel and was thought by some to contain the Holy Grail. However, when it was investigated by Tony Wood and Greg Mills using Groundscan radar, they were unable to find anything inside. What is more likely is that the carvings on the pillar itself form a code communicating one of the secrets of the Holy Grail. Thus, this secret would be preserved for future generations of the Saint Clair branch of the Grail family. As to what this code consists of, there are many theories. Tricks of light and shadow produce for various observers anything from a trembling and pregnant Madonna to an undulating DNA double helix. The apprentice pillar has been said to resemble the Norse Tree of Life, Yggdrasil, the mythological tree which forms a bridge between heaven and hell. It is a bit of a Rorschach test, but most observers would agree that there is definitely something there.

The Apprentice Pillar was built, appropriately enough, by an apprentice stonemason. The story is that the master mason, for whom he was working, went on a trip to Rome to get some inspiration for how to carve the pillar. When he returned, he found that the apprentice had finished it himself, and, what is more, had done an exquisite job. Instead of basking in the reflection of his apprentice's outstanding achievement, he fell into such a rage that he struck the apprentice dead. The story bears an uncanny resemblance to that of the legend of Hiram Abiff, the architect of the Temple of Solomon who was murdered by his apprentice, at least according to Masonic ritual. However, it is reported that the Bishop of St. Andrew made a request to delay the consecration of the building because a violent act had recently taken place during the construction. Also, in the Chapel, there is a carving of a young man, reputed to be the murdered apprentice, with an injury to his face. However, it is possible that this was caused by either accidental or intentional damage.[8]

According to the legend, the master himself also carved a pillar, called "the Mason's Pillar," which can be seen inside the chapel today. An alternate version of the legend states that this pillar is a decoy and that the true Mason's Pillar is in a private garden in Sintra, Portugal. Whether inspired by something he saw in Rome or whether he was competing with his dead apprentice is not known, but his pillar is said to be even more ornate than that of the victim of his rage. Another carving of great interest is that of the inverted

[8] Oliver Cromwell, who had never been much of a respecter of either beauty or tradition (and even banned Christmas celebrations), used the chapel as a stable while he and his troops attacked Roslin Castle in 1650. The damage could also have occurred in 1658, when the chapel was attacked by an angry mob from Edinburgh with some villagers from Roslin, who considered it an example of Roman Catholic excess.

angel. It is positioned at the exact center of the heavily carved eastern wall and is portrayed as being suspended by a rope tied to his legs. It represents Shemhazai who, according to apocryphal legend, played a part in bringing about the great Flood.

In these stories, God was so displeased by the sins that mankind was committing that he regretted having ever made the mischievous animal. Recognizing God's plight, two angels, Azazel and Shemhazai, offered to go down to earth to influence man to behave better. God agreed to this plan, but after a while, as the angels started to mix with the humans, they began to adopt characteristically human wicked ways. Shemhazai even managed to lure 200 angels to cohabit with human women. The children that resulted from these unions influenced men to commit even greater sins. God was naturally incensed by this turn of events, and told Shemhazai that he would send a great flood to destroy the Earth if matters did not improve.

Shemhazai atoned for his sins, but still felt deeply ashamed. He suspended himself upside down between Heaven and Earth so that he would not have to face God.[9] In the meantime, Azazel had no such feelings of contrition. He continued his lascivious ways until God could stand no more and brought about the Flood as a punishment to both man and the fallen angels.

Many will recognize this story as being nearly identical to the story in *The Book of Enoch* about the Fallen Angels referred to as "the Watchers." *The Book of Enoch* was at first accepted by the Christian church, but later rejected. It contained magical and astronomical references. Michael Black, the biblical scholar who has published the most up-to-date analysis of the work, says of *The Book of Enoch*: "What the book presents

---

[9] This may link up with stories that are prevalent throughout many world cultures regarding an heroic god who descends from Heaven on a rope to bestow enlightenment upon mankind such as the Islamic "Marut," the Buddhist "Mura," the Sudanese "Tule" and the East African "Imana." In the Western tradition of the tarot, this image of an angel hanging upside down on a rope is depicted as the "Hanged Man" card.

to the reader is a bizarre variety of disparate and overlapping traditions, containing units of narrative and discourse...The Book of Enoch is like an intricately devised jigsaw puzzle, or rather a collection of such puzzles, in which, after the main component pieces have been put together to make a whole picture, there still remain elements unaccounted for which baffle the most ingenious attempts to fit them into a coherent whole...there is no Ariadne's thread to lead (the reader) through the Enochian Labyrinth." Remnants of the legend about the Watchers can even be found in Genesis 6, where the fallen angels are referred to as "the sons of God" and their unholy progeny "giants," or "nephilim." This is obviously the origin of the tale of the fallen angels led by Lucifer in Milton's Paradise Lost. In fact, the book Rosslyn Chapel by the Earl of Rosslyn explicitly states that the carving of the inverted angel represents Lucifer.

It has been suggested by several researchers that this miscegenation between man and angel is the true origin of the bloodline of the biblical patriarchs, and therefore, the true origin of the European Grail bloodline. Thus, in The Book of Enoch, Noah (an ancestor of Christ) is portrayed as having been one of the offspring of the Watchers. In this account, when Noah is born, he is described as:

> ...a child, the flesh of which was white as snow and red as a rose; the hair of whose head was white like wool, and long; and whose eyes were beautiful. When he opened them, he illuminated all the house, like the sun, the whole house abounded with light.

Noah's father, Lamech, remarks that "he looks not as if he belonged to me, but to the angels."

Interestingly, this story is alluded to in The Da Vinci Code when the character named "Silas," who has albino eyes and snow-white skin, is told by another character:

> Were you not aware that Noah himself was an albino?... Like you, he had skin white like an angel.

The story of *The Book of Enoch* is told both in literal narrative, and in parable. In the latter case, the descent of the fallen angels from Heaven to Earth is symbolized by a star falling from Heaven. This seems to equate with the eminent medieval poet Wolfram von Eschenbach's description of the Grail as being not a cup, but a "stone that fell from Heaven," literally a jewel knocked from Lucifer's crown during the rebellion that descended to Earth. Thereafter it became mankind's most prized possession. In a way, this symbolism represents not only the descent of the angels themselves to Earth, but the *biological* descent of the Grail bloodline from the fallen angels. The symbol of the "stone from Heaven" or the "blazing star" is now central to the mysteries of Freemasonry and of occultism in general.[10] Given this, the fact that "Roslin" may mean "stone falling from Heaven" seems quite significant.

In addition to a variety of Pagan, Christian, Jewish, Masonic and even Luciferian symbolism, there is a great deal of treasure and code at Rosslyn relating to the history of the Saint Clair family itself. When Robert the Bruce died in 1329, William de Saint Clair, the Bishop of Dunkeld, was entrusted with taking his heart, contained in a silver casket, to be buried in Jerusalem. On the way, in Andalusia, King Alfonso of Spain requested the help of his party against the Saracens and William de Saint Clair and his band of knights were massacred. The Saracens were so impressed by the knights' courage that they returned the heart to Scotland (this time in an enamel box), where it was buried at Melrose Abbey (which has a strong Templar history). William de Saint Clair's skull and leg bones were eventually buried at Rosslyn Chapel.

Many researchers have noticed that among the various carvings throughout the chapel depicting plants and foliage, many of the representations are of species (such as maize and aloe vera) that are native only to the Americas and should not have been known to the stonemasons of Rosslyn when the chapel was built, almost fifty years prior to the discoveries of Columbus.

[10] The blazing star symbol can be seen etched above the entrance to the church at Rennes-le-Château.

However, they may have had knowledge of these species through their association with the Saint Clairs. There is a persistent belief among some historians that Henry Saint Clair (a.k.a. "Prince Henry the Navigator") sailed to the Americas in twelve ships as early as 1398. Several traces of this voyage have been left behind. There is still a canon of the type used by the Saint Clair fleet on Cape Breton Island, Nova Scotia. The grave of one of Henry Saint Clair's knights can be seen at Westford, Massachusetts, and there is an effigy there of a fourteenth century knight carved into a rock ledge. There is also a two-story circular medieval tower of Scottish design in Newport, Rhode Island. Its bears a strong resemblance to the twelfth century Orphir Chapel on Orkney, and it was built in the style of the Knights Templar.

There is a peculiar legend stating that when a member of the Saint Clair family dies, a glow spreads throughout the stones of Rosslyn Chapel. The last report of this happening was when a younger member of the family was killed in action five days after the outbreak of the Second World War.[11] Sir Walter Scott wrote of this phenomenon in his poem *The Lay of the Minstrel*, which says:

> *O'er Roslin all that dreary night,*
> *A wondrous blaze was seen to gleam;*
> *'Twas broader than the watch-fire's light,*
> *And redder than the bright moon-beam.*

The most fascinating stories about Rosslyn Chapel tell of treasure of some kind being hidden there. A crypt has been found with the same depth and height as that of the Chapel, but is accessible at the moment only by a very old staircase and it is filled with fine sand. William Saint Clair ("the Seemly") brought from the Holy Land the "Holy" or "Blood Rood" which is purportedly part of the true cross and saturated with Christ's blood. This is the relic after which Holyrood House and Abbey were named.

[11] The incident is apparently quite reliably reported. The member of the family who was killed was on active service in the RAF (the British Royal Air Force).

The Holy Rood and the Stone of Scone are considered to be the most valuable artifacts among the Scottish coronation treasures. Sir William Sinclair saved many of the Scottish treasures during the Reformation and it is thought that he hid them at Rosslyn Chapel. If this is the case, it is more than likely that they are still in the crypt today. Additionally, some of the Templar treasure which was brought from France to Scotland during the Catholic Inquisition is thought to be contained within this crypt. It may also be home to the scrolls of the Zadok priests of first century Jerusalem. This is perhaps the most valuable type of treasure that Rosslyn Chapel could conceivably reveal to us. Perhaps this is what Sir William Sinclair was referring to when he inscribed the following in Latin on a lintel next to the Apprentice Pillar:

"Wine is strong, a King is stronger, women are even stronger, but TRUTH conquers all."

Chapter Thirteen
London

The Temple Church

As Dan Brown tells us in *The Da Vinci Code*, the Temple Church dates back to 1185. However, although the ground plan of the original structure remains unchanged, the restorers, and particularly those of the nineteenth century, have ensured that, as the architect Walter Godfrey said, "every ancient surface was removed or renewed." It is thought that the church, which was built by the Knights Templar at the same time as their great house, was modeled not on the Holy Sepulchre in Jerusalem, as Brown claims, but on the circular design of the Dome of the Rock.

The church is built in what is known as the Transitional style. Purbeck marble, from Dorset in southern England, has been used liberally. The consecration of the church was carried out by Heraclius, the Patriarch of Jerusalem, in the presence of King Henry II and it was dedicated to the Blessed Mary. A small chapel was built which was dedicated to St. Anne. All that remains of it now is its crypt in which secret initiation ceremonies were performed. In 1950 another basement chapel was found which is thought to be the Knights Templars' treasury. The church also has a penitential cell where Walter-le-Bachelor, the Grand Preceptor of Ireland, was left to starve to death for having disobeyed the Master of the Order.

Following the decline of the Templars in the fourteenth century, their property was handed over to the Knights Hospitallers who leased the Temple to lawyers until Henry VIII took the property over. King James I gave the freehold of the church to lawyers on condition that they maintained it and its services forever. To this day, the appointment of the chaplain or Master is the prerogative of the Monarch and not the Bishop of London.

Sir Christopher Wren, to whom Dan Brown refers as "the Temple Church's most famous benefactor," was called upon to "beautify" the church in 1682 and this is when the battlements and buttresses were added. At this time the church was being used by lawyers and a clerk of the Temple, John Playford, set up a music shop in the West Porch where Samuel Pepys, the famous diarist, bought sheet music of the latest songs.

Much of the refurbishment that took place in the nineteenth century was destroyed in the Blitz, and therefore, contrary to what Brown writes, the church did not come through the Second World War unscathed. Several of the figures of the Crusader knights which had lain in the church were also damaged, but they have been well restored. The east windows were also destroyed in the bombing.

There are four "Inns of Court" in London – Lincoln's Inn (founded in 1422), Middle Temple (1501), Inner Temple (1505), and Gray's Inn (1569). They have the exclusive right of admitting people to the English bar and each is referred to as an "Honourable Society." King James I gave the freehold of the church to the lawyers – the southern half to those of the Inner Temple and the northern half to those of the Middle Temple. The condition was that they maintain the church and its services in perpetuity. To this day it is the custom for the barristers of the Inner Temple and the Middle Temple to occupy their respective halves of the church.

Westminster Abbey

A church has stood on the present site of Westminster Abbey in London since the seventh century, when King Sebert of the East Saxons founded it. At that time it would have been built on Thorney Island. Now the island does not exist as the

Thames has narrowed, absorbing the island into the mainland. The church was apparently founded on the instructions of St. Peter, who appeared at the consecration of the Church by Melitus, its first bishop. The church is shown in the Bayeaux Tapestry to have a central tower, transepts and a lead roof.

The Abbey was built by Edward the Confessor and consecrated in 1065. To honor Edward, Henry III vowed to build a more impressive Abbey in the Gothic style, leaving only a few parts of the original structure. From the thirteenth to the sixteenth centuries, English kings contributed to the design with the result that it has become a hodgepodge of styles. In this way it rather resembles the present British royal family, which also originates from a large number of sources and which has long used the Abbey as a "parish church" for weddings, coronations, and funerals. However, as Dan Brown tells us in *The Da Vinci Code*, the Abbey's identity is that of neither a cathedral nor a parish church, but is what is known as a "royal peculiar" under the jurisdiction of a Dean and Chapter, subject only to the Sovereign. The entrance is at the side of the church, in the North Transept, although on the abbey's floor plan, it appears to be on the left-hand side.

King Edward the Confessor dedicated the church to St. Peter at the request of Pope Leo IX. William I (the Conqueror) of Normandy, France was the first King to be crowned in the abbey. He defeated the English King Harold at the Battle of Hastings. The coronation took place on Christmas Day 1066 and the native English gathered around the door shouting their praises. The jumpy Normans misinterpreted this and William was quaking in fear for his life throughout the ceremony. After the coronation, the Normans attacked the crowds and set fire to some buildings. This did nothing to improve Anglo-French relations, which have always been on the shaky side.

Since this time, all British monarchs have had their coronations at Westminster Abbey, with the exceptions of Edward

V and Edward VIII. Many are also buried there. The new building of the church was influenced greatly by churches that King Henry III had seen in France, such as those at Amiens, of which it is particularly reminiscent, and Saint-Chapelle in Paris. It was, in fact, described by Antoine Pevsner, the Russian-born French painter and sculptor, as the "most French of all English Gothic churches."

Much of the church, including the Chapter House, was completed by 1254. In 1413 Henry IV had a fit in the Abbey while he was praying, and was carried into the Jerusalem Chapel where he died. In *Henry IV, Part II*, Shakespeare mentions this and, for added effect, shows Prince Henry trying on the crown while his father lay dying.

In 1540 the monastery was dissolved and the funding that the Abbey would have received was transferred to St. Paul's Cathedral; hence the expression "robbing Peter to pay Paul." At this point, the Abbey became a cathedral. The soldiers of Oliver Cromwell, who had Charles I executed and ruled England as Lord Protector from 1653-8, later occupied the Abbey. There they "broke down the rails before the Table and burnt them in the very place in the heat of July but wretchedly profaned the very Table itself by setting about it with their tobacco and all before them." Cromwell was also buried in the Abbey, but during the Restoration his body was dug up, beheaded and buried at the foot of the gallows at the traditional hanging venue of Tyburn, near what is now Marble Arch in London.

In the late seventeenth and early eighteenth centuries, Sir Christopher Wren, who designed so many of London's churches following the Great Fire of 1666, restored parts of the Abbey. From the eighteenth century onwards, so many monuments and statues were erected in the Abbey that the actual architectural form of the Abbey has become obscured.

The tomb of Sir Isaac Newton

As we know from *The Da Vinci Code*, Sir Isaac Newton is buried at Westminster Abbey. He is in good and illustrious company.

The English dramatist and lawyer, Francis Beaumont (1584 – 1616), who is also buried in the Abbey wrote:

Think how many royal bones
Sleep within these heaps of stones
Here they lie, had realms and lands
Who now want strength to stir their hands.

At the time that he wrote this, most of those who were buried at the Abbey were of royal blood. The earliest are said to be of King Sebert and his wife. It was King Richard II who started the practice of burying distinguished commoners in the Abbey and since that time many high-ranking warriors, scientists, musicians, poets, clergy, politicians and reformers have found their final resting place here. Geoffrey Chaucer was the first poet to be buried in the Abbey in 1400. Ben Johnson, the contemporary of William Shakespeare and fellow poet, is also buried here. It is said that Johnson asked for a grave in the Abbey, but was impoverished and did not want to give the impression that he was asking for too much. Therefore he said, "Six feet by two feet wide is too much for me; two feet and two feet do for all I want." So he was buried standing up.

In the part of the Abbey known as Poets' Corner, most of the poets who are commemorated here are not buried in the Abbey. In fact many of them were considered to lead wasteful and decadent lives and in such cases it was not until several years after their deaths that they were deemed worthy of commemoration at all.

The monument to Sir Isaac Newton is in the area known as Scientists' Corner. It was designed by William Kent (1685 – 1748) and sculpted by Michael Rysbrack (1694 – 1770). It is made of white and grey marble. The sarcophagus has a panel showing boys using Newton's mathematical instruments. Above the sarcophagus there is a reclining figure representing Newton with his right elbow leaning on several of his better known works. With his left hand he points to a scroll depicting a mathematical design which is held by two boys. In the background there is a globe which shows the astrological signs of the zodiac and the constellations and it traces the path of the comet which appeared in 1680.

The Latin inscription on the monument translates as follows:

> Here is buried Isaac Newton, Knight, who by a strength of mind almost divine and mathematical principles peculiarly his own explored the course and figures of the planets, the paths of the comets, the tides of the seas, the dissimilarities in rays of light, and, what no other scholar has previously imagined, the properties of the colours thus produced. Diligent, sagacious and faithful in his expositions of nature, antiquity and the holy Scriptures, he vindicated by his philosophy the majesty of God mighty and good, and expressed the simplicity of the Gospel in his manners. Mortals rejoice that there has existed such and so great an ornament of the human race! He was born on 25th December 1642 and died on 20th March 1726/7.

> (Translation from G.L. Smyth The Monuments and Genii of St. Paul's Cathedral, and of Westminster Abbey (1826), ii 703-4)

Newton was buried at the Abbey on March 28, 1727 and had an honored funeral. He lay in state in the Jerusalem Chapel and most of the Fellows of the Royal Society attended the funeral. His pall bearers were the Lord Chancellor, two dukes and three earls.

The Chapter House

The Chapter House is situated in the East Cloister. It was built from 1245 – 1255 and was the location of the Great Council of King Henry III on March 26, 1257. It was also used from the middle of the fourteenth century until 1547 between the reigns of Edward I and Henry VIII, as the House of Commons. For that reason the Chapter House is not under the control of the Dean and Chapter, but belongs to the Crown. After that it was used to store documents until 1866. It is an octagonal building housing some beautiful but worn sculptures. It has a reputation for having one of the finest tile floors in England.

The Cloisters

Before the Reformation, the Cloisters were a center of great activity in the monastic Abbey. They were used for meditation and exercise, as well as for access to other parts of the monastery. In those days, the East Cloister was used as the place where the Abbot used to hold what was called "the Maundy." It occurred on the Thursday before Easter Sunday and the ceremony involved the Abbot washing the feet of thirteen elderly monks. The day is still known as Maundy Thursday. It is the day when the Sovereign gives Maundy Money (in pounds and pence) to old soldiers known as the Chelsea Pensioners, who live in Chelsea Royal Hospital on King's Road. In pre-Reformation days the Abbot gave each man three pence, seven red herrings, some ale and three loaves of bread. At the same time, in the South Walk in a similar demonstration of humility, monks washed the feet of children where you can still see their Maundy seat, "a faire, long bench of stone."

St. Faith's Chapel

This building was named after a third century virgin who was martyred for being a Christian by being roasted over a gridiron. She was a cult figure in England and France in the thirteenth century and the Chapel was built in the 1250s. There is a thirteenth century wall painting here of St. Faith wearing a crown and holding the implement of her martyrdom, the gridiron.

The Pyx Chamber

The Chamber was built between 1065 and 1090, and was probably made into a treasury in the thirteenth century. It was probably also used as a sacristy during the time of Henry III during the rebuilding of the main Abbey. The tiled floor depicts mainly heraldic subjects. During the time of Edward I, the Pyx Chamber formed part of the Royal Wardrobe, but it was burgled in 1303 while the King was in Scotland and money and silver plate were stolen. Because of this, the present double-oak security doors at the Chamber entrance were built, and provided enough security for the storage of valuables which belonged to the

Exchequer. The two large rectangular chests in the Chamber, dating from the thirteenth and fourteenth centuries, must have been constructed inside the room.

The main purpose of the Pyx Chamber came to be housing wooden boxes where samples of the coinage were kept, awaiting what was known as the "Trial of the Pyx." This was a public demonstration of the purity of the metal used in the coinage, in which sample coins were melted down and the silver content measured. The Trial itself was held in the Palace of Westminster and is still carried out to this day at Goldsmiths' Hall in the City of London.

Glossary

Ark of the Covenant: known in Hebrew as Aron Ha-berit. It represents the heavily ornate, gold-plated wooden chest that traditionally contained the two tablets of the Law in biblical times given to Moses by God, and is sacred to both Judaism and Christianity. The Ark was kept in the part of the Tabernacle of the ancient Temple of Jerusalem known as the Holy of Holies. It was permitted to be seen only by the high priest of the Israelites on Yom Kippur, the Day of Atonement. The Ark was carried by the Levites (who were the priestly officials) while the Hebrews were wandering in the desert. The Israelites sometimes took it with them into battle. King David took it to Jerusalem, and eventually King Saul placed it in the Temple of Solomon. Its present whereabouts are unknown.

Baphomet: The word "Baphomet" could be a corruption of "Mahomet" or "Mohammed" in English, the Muslim prophet. Some say that the word comes from the joining of two Greek words meaning "absorption into wisdom." During their persecution, the Knights Templar were accused of worshipping an idol named Baphomet, to which they admitted under torture. It was said to take the form of either a head or a black cat. It is believed that the imagery of the Baphomet derives from the ancient Egyptian god Amon, meaning "The Hidden One," who is also known as the Goat of Mendes. Eliphas Lévi, the nineteenth century occultist, described some of the more common and varied descriptions of Baphomet in various combinations of animal and human heads, and, perhaps most significantly with the head of a goat and the body of a man, but with wings and cloven feet (the Sabbatic Goat.) This concept of the Sabbatic Goat led to the present-day perception of the devil. Not only the British occultist, Aleister Crowley, but also Church of Satan founder, Anton LaVey, adopted the Baphomet imagery. When the Templars' Paris preceptory was raided another Baphomet head was found bearing the legend "Caput 58M." It is reasonable to assume that when you add the two digits five and eight and reach thirteen, the combination of the two digits and the letter referred to Mary Magdalene, as "M" is the thirteenth letter of the alphabet. The origin of the Baphomet has also been ascribed to the head of John the Baptist, who was considered by the Templars to be the true messiah, in favor of Christ who was considered to be false. The Eliphas Lévi image of the Baphomet now represents the Devil in the Waite version of the Tarot cards as the androgynous half male, half female, half human, half animal.

Bergers d'Arcadie, Les: When Bérenger Saunière visited Paris with the parchments that he had found in Rennes-le-Château, he bought reproductions of three paintings. One of these was the picture Les Bergers d'Arcadie (The Shepherds of Arcadia) by Nicolas Poussin. It had a history. Abbé Louis Fouquet, was the brother of Nicholas, the Superintendent of Finances to Louis XIV of France, and he paid Nicolas Poussin a visit in 1656 while Poussin was living in Rome. Shortly afterwards, the Abbé wrote to his brother saying that he had discovered secrets that would give him, through Poussin, "advantages which even kings would have great pains to draw" from him and which, according to him, it is possible that nobody else will ever rediscover in the centuries to come. The enigma of this mystery remains, but shortly after he received the letter, Nicholas Fouquet was arrested and imprisoned for the rest of his life. The King, Louis XIV went to great lengths to buy the painting, Les Bergers d'Arcadie, and kept it hidden in the Palace of Versailles. The picture consists of three shepherds and a shepherdess looking at a tomb on which is written the inscription "ET IN ARCADIA EGO." It was generally considered that the tomb and the landscape in which it is located were products of Poussin's imagination. However, in the 1970s an identical tomb was found, in an identical landscape, six miles from

Rennes-le-Château. The tomb had been there for as long as the local people could remember, and there is apparently a mention of it in a memoir dating back to 1709. Baigent, Leigh and Lincoln received a possible explanation for the inscription on the tomb from one of their TV viewers. It is an intriguing anagram of the Latin:

I TEGO ARCANA DEI
(BEGONE! I CONCEAL THE SECRETS OF GOD)

It is said in the documents of the Priory of Sion that "Et in Arcadia Ego" was also the official device of the Plantard family from the twelfth century. David Wood and Ian Campbell in *Poussin's Secret* say that Professor Cornford analyzed *Les Bergers d'Arcadie* in the BBC Chronicle film *The Priest, the Painter and the Devil*, in which he pointed out the construction of the painting being a combination of the Golden Section and Pentagonal geometry. This pentangle is centered on the womb of the shepherdess. The churches and other important features in the Rennes-le-Château area also form such a pentagram.

Cana, the wedding feast: Cana was a small ancient town in Galilee where Christ attended a marriage feast during which he is said to have performed the first miracle of changing water into wine. Mary also attended the wedding feast, and she asked Jesus to replenish the supply of wine. Mary told the servants to do whatever Jesus wants them to do. The servants responded as if they felt it natural for Jesus and Mary to give them orders. However, it seems improbable that two guests at a wedding feast would take upon themselves the responsibility of the ensuring that there was sufficient wine. It also seems unlikely that Jesus would use this opportunity to perform his first miracle as some kind of "party trick." It is far more likely that this was the marriage of Jesus, and he was responsible for providing more wine. Also, the Gospel of St. John 2:9-10 reports that the "Governor of the Feast," whose role was perhaps similar to that of the present-day Best Man, tastes the wine: "the governor of the feast called the bridegroom. And saith unto him, Every man at the beginning doth set forth good wine; and when the men have well drunk, then that which is worse; but thou has kept the good wine till now." He must have been addressing Jesus as the provider of the wine, and therefore the bridegroom.

Cathars: (from Greek katharos, "pure") is also written "Cathari." They were considered heretics in the Middle Ages. They practiced a form of neo-Manichaean dualism which believed that the world was ruled by two equally powerful gods. One was the spiritual and "good god" or the God of Love. The other god represented the material world which was fundamentally evil, and he was known as "Rex Mundi" or "King of the World." This was at odds with Catholicism which maintained that even though evil comes from the Devil, it becomes apparent through man and his actions. The Cathars abhorred the riches and wealth of the Catholic Church, and preferred to live a life of denial. Because they believed that matter was evil, they denied that Jesus could consume material as a man and still be the Son of God. They saw him as being no different from any other man who was crucified. Some believed that Jesus was just a pure spirit who could not possibly be able to suffer and die. They also believed that procreation was wrong, although they stopped short of banning sex, no doubt for practical reasons from every point of view. They were fish-eating "vegetarians." From the 1140s the Cathars were an organized church with a hierarchy, a liturgy, and a system of doctrine. Its popularity in France and Italy perhaps led to its downfall. Eventually Pope Innocent III (1198 – 1216) tried to get Raymond VI, count of Toulouse, to help him put down the heresy. However, it went badly wrong. The representative of the Pope was murdered in January 1208, and the Count was suspected of being an accessory to the crime. Therefore in 1209 the Albigensian Crusade was organized to deal with the Cathars. An army of about 30,000 attacked the southern French region of Languedoc, and massacred all in their wake as well as destroying the crops, towns and cities. The last stronghold of the Cathars, Montsegur, fell in 1244. Some think that the Cathars were party to a secret and/or the guardians of a great treasure which they managed to smuggle out of Montsegur.

Constantine, the Donation of: *The Donation of Constantine* appeared in the eighth century – created supposedly four hundred years before it was found. The Roman Church claimed that it had been written by Emperor Constantine the Great to Pope Sylvester, presumably before Constantine's death in 337 AD. It was to express Constantine's gratitude to the Pope for having cured him of leprosy. In recognition and acknowledgement of his thanks, he transferred the entire power of the Holy Roman Empire to the Church. This included the right to select and deselect monarchs. Lorenzo Valla tested its authenticity during the Renaissance, and found evidence that it could not have been written at the time of Constantine. However, although *the Donation of Constantine* was proven to be a fraud, the Church has never admitted so, and has continued to wield the rights that it gained illegitimately.

Desposyni, the (the descendants of Christ): According to the close friend of Constantine the Great, the Bishop Eusebius, the historian Julius Africanus who lived in the period AD 160 – 240, wrote, "Herod, who had no drop of Israelitish blood in his veins and was stung by the consciousness of his base origins, burnt the registers of their families ... A few careful people had private records of their won, having either remembered the names or recovered them from copies, and took pride in preserving the memory of their aristocratic origin. These included the people ... known as Desposyni (meaning the Master's People) because of their relationship to the savior's family." St. Paul himself said that he had married, and was, in fact, a widower. There is no record of the brother of Jesus, James, having had any children. However, he was a truly devout Jew, and would therefore have without doubt married, as it was the law. Again according to Eusebius, the descendants of Jesus' family, including, perhaps, those of Jesus himself, became leaders of various Christian churches, and followed rules of strict dynastic succession. He traces them back to the era of Emperor Trojan, that is AD 98 – 117. During the time of Constantine, in AD 318, a deputation of the Desposyni met Pope Sylvester to make various demands of him, including the resumption of funds being sent to their church in Jerusalem, and its recognition as the Mother Church. Needless to say, all their demands were rejected. The Mother Church was, for better or worse, well established in Rome by that time, and there was no question of that situation changing.

Holy Grail: referred to in early manuscripts as Sangraal, and, it was spelled by Sir Thomas Malory (the writer of *Le Morte d'Arthur* printed in 1483), as Sangreal. It is probable that one of these versions was the original. The word can clearly be split into either San Graal (meaning "Holy Grail"), or Sang Real (meaning "Royal Blood"), referring to the bloodline of Jesus Christ which led to the Merovingian dynasty. Alternatively, there is the chalice, known as the Holy Grail, that the Catholic Church recognizes as that which was used by Jesus Christ at the Last Supper, and which the Popes in Rome used until St. Lawrence took it to Spain. It can now be seen in Valencia Cathedral in Spain

Knights Templar: The Knights Templar were founded in 1188, the same year as the possibly allegorical tale of the "Cutting of the Elm" which describes some sort of split or rift. Whether or not this has anything to do with the Priory of Sion and the Knights Templar, the Priory of Sion documents describes the new-found independence of the Templars from the Priory, and the beginning of their autonomy from 1188. The purpose of the Knights Templar was ostensibly to protect pilgrims on their way to the Holy Land. The quarters that they were given were on the site of Solomon's Temple in Jerusalem. This is perhaps of special significance, as it would have given the Templars the opportunity to investigate any secret that the site had to offer. The order became so wealthy that Philip the Fair of France (Philip IV) felt increasingly threatened by them – he also owed them a large amount of money. He persuaded Pope Clement V to join with him in the persecution of the Knights Templar, and this began on Friday, October 13, 1307, when their property was confiscated, and the Knights Templar were tortured into making various confessions, including "devil worship," after which they were brutally executed.

Merovingians: thought to be the monarchs that descended, through the Davidic line, from the descendants of Jesus Christ who arrived in France with Mary Magdalene. It was a dynasty that reigned in Gaul and present-day Germany from about 500 – 750, and their lands were gradually extended as their success and prosperity grew. After the controversial assassination of King Dagobert II, the impression was given that the line had died out, and it was replaced by their former servants – "Mayors of the Palace" – who formed the Carolingian line. These monarchs, including Charlemagne, married Merovingian princesses themselves, thus keeping the Davidic line alive.

Opus Dei: (in full, Prelature of the Holy Cross and Opus Dei) is a controversial Roman Catholic organization consisting of laymen and priests. It was founded in Spain in 1928 by Josemaría Escrivá de Balaguer y Albás who was canonized in 2002. Some members of Opus Dei, who are known as numeraries, devote themselves wholeheartedly to the organization. They are required to remain unmarried and to take vows of celibacy, obedience, and chastity, but they live in the world and pursue secular occupations; they are known to practice self-mortification. Others are allowed to marry, and contribute to the organization financially. Several members were involved in the economic reforms implemented by Generalissimo Franco, the fascist Spanish dictator, in 1956. After Franco's death in 1975, the influence of Opus Dei in Spain lessened, although it is still popular there. Opus Dei denies the frequent accusations leveled against it of aggressive recruiting practices, including the brainwashing of new recruits, and the isolation of members from their families.

Pierre Plantard de Saint-Clair: re-established the Priory of Sion in 1956. He was the last alleged Grand Master of the Priory of Sion, and was interviewed several times by Baigent, Leigh and Lincoln for their books *Holy Blood, Holy Grail* and *The Messianic Legacy*. In 1979, when he was Secretary-General, he told them that the Priory of Sion possessed the treasure from the Temple of Jerusalem which had been plundered by the Romans during the revolt of AD 66 and eventually taken perhaps to the south of France, near Rennes-le-Château. He also said that the treasure would be returned to Israel when the "time was right." Apparently he took up the office of Grand Master on January 17, 1981, and stepped down in 1984. It is not known who was in office between him and Jean Cocteau, who had died in 1963.

Priory of Sion: a secret society that dates back to the twelfth century. Its history can be traced until the sixteenth century, but seemed to go underground in about 1619 when it appeared to operate under different names, and sometimes disappeared entirely. The modern form of the organization was re-founded in 1956 by Pierre Plantard de Saint-Clair and some of his associates. It was officially disbanded in 1984. The purpose of the organization is thought to be to protect and promote the interests of the Merovingian dynasty that the Priory considered to be the rightful rulers of Europe.

Rosicrucians: There is no evidence of the Rosicrucians existing before at least the end of the sixteenth century. The earliest document that mentions it is the *Fama Fraternitatis* ("Account of the Brotherhood"), first published in 1614. The organization devoted itself to the study of metaphorical and mystical lore, and they were particularly interested in the transmutation of metals, the lengthening of life, and control of the elements. Its name comes from the combination of the rose and the cross. The movement is said to have been founded by a mythical fifteenth century knight, Christian Rosenkreuz, who was allegedly born in 1378 and lived for 106 years. The story is that he acquired esoteric wisdom when traveling in Egypt, Damascus, Damcar in Arabia, and Fès in Morocco. He then handed on this knowledge to others when he returned to Germany. He is thought to have had eight disciples who spread his knowledge throughout the world. These days the name is used by similarly focused groups.

Saunière, Bérenger: appointed to the church of the village of Rennes-le-Château in the area of southern France known as

Languedoc, in 1855. The village church had been dedicated to Mary Magdalene. One of the first tasks Saunière set himself was the refurbishment of the church. During this he found parchments hidden in a pillar which appeared to be in code. He took them to show his Bishop who sent him immediately to Paris. There he met Abbé Bieil, the Director General of Saint-Sulpice, and his nephew, a well-respected scholar of linguistics and cryptography. He also met many celebrities of the day during these three weeks he spent in Paris. Once he returned to Rennes-le-Château, he decorated the church with a confusing mixture of ambiguous imagery, and placed a statue of Asmodeus, "Rex Mundi" in the entrance. He adopted strange habits, such as walking around the countryside collecting stones and rocks. He was also visited by various important people, and suddenly became very rich. He built a house next to the church, and a tower on the mountainside, as well as paying for a road that led up the mountain to the village. He died in mysterious circumstances in 1916, and his housekeeper lived on in the house until her death, perhaps taking his secret to the grave.

References And Recommended Further Reading And Viewing

Publications

Michael Baigent, Richard Leigh and Henry Lincoln, *Holy Blood, Holy Grail*, New York: Dell, 1983

Michael Baigent, Richard Leigh and Henry Lincoln, *The Messianic Legacy*, New York: Dell, 1989

Michael Baigent and Richard Leigh, *The Dead Sea Scrolls Deception*, New York: Simon & Schuster, 1993

Tracy Twyman and Boyd Rice, *The Vessel of God*, York Beach, ME: Weiser Books, 2004

Nicholas de Vere, *The Dragon Legacy*, San Diego, CA.: The Book Tree, 2004

Ean and Deike Begg, *In Search of the Holy Grail and the Precious Blood*, Thorsons, London: 1995

Laurence Gardner, *Bloodline of the Holy Grail*, Gloucester, MA, Fair Winds Press, 2002

Christopher Knight and Robert Lomas, *Uriel's Machine, The Ancient Origins of Science*, London: Arrow, 2000

Alison Weir, *Britain's Royal Families*, London: Pimlico, 2002

James M. Robinson, ed., *The Nag Hammadi Library in English*, San Francisco, CA: HarperCollins 1990, pp. 139-160, Wesley W. Isenberg writes p. 141

Bentley Layton, *The Gnostic Scriptures, Ancient Wisdom for the New Age*, Anchor Bible Reference Library – ABRL, Doubleday, 1987

Geoffrey Ash, *Mythology of the British Isles*, London: Methuen, 1990

David Wood and Ian Campbell, *Poussin's Secret*, Tunbridge Wells, England: Genisis Trading Co. Ltd., 1995

HRH Prince Michael of Alban, *The Forgotten Monarchy of Scotland*, London: Element, 1998

Ben Weinreb and Christopher Hibbert, *The London Encyclopaedia*, London: Papermac, 1983

Joseph Maxwell, *The Tarot*, London: Neville Spearman, 1975

Ivor H. Evans, *Brewer's Dictionary of Phrase and Fable*, New York: HarperResource, 2000

Robert Graves, *The Greek Myths*, New York: Penguin USA, 1993

Christopher Haigh (editor), *The Cambridge Historical Encyclopedia of Great Britain and Ireland*, London: Cambridge University Press, 1985

Tracy Twyman, *Dagobert's Revenge Magazine*

Television Programs

ABC News *Primetime Monday, Jesus, Mary, and Da Vinci* (features interview with Dan Brown among other interesting information)

Discovery Civilization, *The Real Jesus Christ*

Discovery Civilization, *The Holy Grail*

Henry Lincoln has produced a number of relevant documentaries for the BBC, including:

- *The Lost Treasure of Jerusalem* (1972)
- *The Devil's Hoard of Rennes-le-Château* (1973)
- *The Priest, the Painter and the Devil* (1974)
- *The Shadow of the Templars* (1979)

There are also two video documentaries featuring Henry Lincoln, both distributed by Illuminated Word in the UK, entitled *Henry Lincoln's Guide to Rennes-Le-Château and the Aude Valley* (2000) and *The Secret*, made in 1992 and subsequently broadcast on the Discovery Channel in a cut version as *The Secrets of the Templars*. See www.tour-magdala.com for details.

On the Web

www.thedavincicode.com *The Da Vinci Code's* publisher bills it as "the most fun you've ever had on the web." For readers of this book the game should be a cinch.

www.dagobertsrevenge.com The online version of Tracy Twyman's invaluable *Dagobert's Revenge* magazine.

www.opusdei.org The official website of Opus Dei.

www.odan.org Dianne DiNicola's Opus Dei Awareness Network.

www.templarhistory.com The online version of Stephen Dafoe's *Templar History* magazine.

www.danbrown.com Among other resources available on his website, Dan Brown supplies a partial bibliography for *The Da Vinci Code*. It partially overlaps with the references cited above, but is reproduced below in its entirety. Mr. Brown does not supply dates or publisher information and this list has not been modified by the author or publisher of this book.

The History of the Knights Templars
– Charles G. Addison

Rosslyn: *Guardians of the Secret of the Holy Grail*
– Tim Wallace-Murphy

The Woman With The Alabaster Jar: Mary Magdalene and the Holy Grail
– Margaret Starbird

The Templar Revelation: Secret Guardians of the True Identity of Christ
– Lynn Picknett & Clive Prince

The Goddess in the Gospels: Reclaiming the Sacred Feminine
– Margaret Starbird

Holy Blood, Holy Grail
– Michael Baigent, Richard Leigh, Henry Lincoln

The Search for the Holy Grail and the Precious Blood
– Deike Begg

The Messianic Legacy
– Michael Baigent

The Knights Templar and their Myth
– Peter Partner

The Dead Sea Bible. The Oldest Known Bible
– Martin G. Abegg

The Dead Sea Deception
– Michael Baigent, Richard Leigh, Henry Lincoln

The Nag Hammadi Library in English
– James M. Robinson

Jesus and the Lost Goddess: The Secret Teachings of the Original Christians
– Timothy Freke, Peter Gandy

When God was a Woman

– Merlin Stone
The Chalice and the Blade. Our History, our Future
– Riane Eisler

Born in Blood
– John J. Robinson

The Malleus Maleficarum
– Heinrich Kramer & James Sprenger

The Notebooks of Leonardo da Vinci
– Leonardo da Vinci

Prophecies
– Leonardo da Vinci

Leonardo da Vinci: Scientist, Inventor, Artist
– Otto Letze

Leonardo: The Artist and the Man
– Serge Bramly, Sian Reynolds

Their Kingdom Come: Inside the secret world of Opus Dei
– Robert A. Hutchison

Beyond the Threshold: A Life in Opus Dei
– Maria Del Carmen Tapia

The Pope's Armada: Unlocking the Secrets of Mysterious and Powerful New
Sects in the Church
– Gordon Urguhart

Opus Dei: An Investigation into the Secret Society Struggling for Power
Within the Roman Catholic Church – Michael Walsh

I. M. Pei: A Profile in American Architecture
– Carter Wiseman

Conversations With I. M. Pei: Light Is the Key
– Gero Von Boehm

Index

A

Adoration of the Magi, the, 7, 18-19
anatomy studies, by Leonardo, 7-8, 19
Algeria, 44-45
Apprentice Pillar, the, 143-144, 149
Arcadia, Greece, 50
Arius, 84, 98
Arians, the, 98
Arthur, King, 52, 54, 89-92
Atbash Cipher, 119-120
Avalon, 89
Asmodeus, 71, 167

B

Baigent, Leigh, and Lincoln, 24, 26-27, 34, 42-43, 46, 61,
79, 120, 127, 161, 165
Balaguer, Msgr. Josemaría Escrivá de, 112
Baphomet, 29, 120-123, 159-160
Benjamite tribe, the, 57
Bethlehem, 101
Bilderberg Group, the, 126
Blanchefort, Bertrand de, 30, 61, 67, 74
blasphemy, 22, 103
bloodlines, Davidic and Merovingian, 49, 51, 53, 55, 57,
59, 61, 63, 65
Borgia, Cesare, the Duke of Valentinois, 9
Botticelli, 7, 39

D

E

F

G

M

N

O

P

S

T

U

V

W

About the Author

Martin Lunn is a recognized expert in the Davidic bloodline and other issues presented in *The Da Vinci Code*. He has a Masters degree in History and an extensive background in journalism. He has lived throughout the Far and Middle East, the US and several countries in Europe, currently residing in Barcelona. He is also Grand Master of the Dragon Society, founded originally in 1408 by King Sigismund of Hungary.